MIMESIS
INTERNATIONAL

SOCIOLOGY
n. 8

ILARIA RICCIONI

FUTURISM: ANTICIPATING POSTMODERNISM

A Sociological Essay on Avant-garde Art and Society

Foreword by
Franco Ferrarotti

MIMESIS
INTERNATIONAL

Originally published as *Futurismo, logica del postmoderno. Saggio su arte e società*. Copyright 2003 Editrice La Mandragora, Imola (Bo), Italy

Translation into English by Alex Gillan and Ilaria Riccioni

© 2019 – MIMESIS INTERNATIONAL
www.mimesisinternational.com
e-mail: info@mimesisinternational.com

Book series: *Sociology*, n. 8

Isbn: 9788869772313

© MIM Edizioni Srl
P.I. C.F. 0241937030

TABLE OF CONTENTS

FOREWORD. ART AND SOCIETY
by Franco Ferrarotti   7

INTRODUCTION TO THE ENGLISH EDITION   9

INTRODUCTION. FUTURISM: ANTICIPATING A NEW SOCIAL ACTION   13

CHAPTER I
THE SOCIAL ROLE OF ART:
RELATIONS AND INTERTWINING IN ART AND SOCIETY   21

  I.1 THE BREAKDOWN IMPLICIT IN THE ARRIVAL OF INDUSTRIAL SOCIETY   21
    I.1.a   The Concept of Avant-garde Art   21
    I.1.b   The Escape from History   24
    I.1.c   Novelty and the Avant-garde   38
    I.1.d   Theories of the Avant-garde   50
  I.2 THE MODERN AND POSTMODERN IN ART   53

CHAPTER II
THE ARTISTIC ACTION AS A SOCIAL PROPOSAL:
FUTURISM AND THE DOMINATION OF TECHNIQUE   61

  II.1 THEORY OF FUTURISM AND SOCIOLOGICAL ISSUES   61
    II.1.a   Art as Place of Conflict   61
    II.1.b   The Dialectic between Societal
        and Individual Changes   65
    II.1.c   Organizing Social Action through Analogy
        and Intuition   68
    II.1.d   Critique of Modernism   72
  II.2 FUTURISM AND POLITICS   78

CHAPTER III
AN AUTHORITARIAN ACTION:
THE HISTORICAL TIES OF FUTURISM   93

III.1 THE PREMISES OF A NEW SOCIAL ORDER   93

III.2 SOCIAL CONSTRUCTION OF A NEW MASS AWARENESS:
       THE MEDIUM OF MANIFESTOS   107

       III.2.a Analysis of the Manifestos   109
       III.2.b Art as Energy   115
       III.2.c The Moving Image   118
       III.2.d Manifesto of the Futurist Woman   130
       III.2.e The Technical Manifesto of Futurist Literature   139

CHAPTER IV   141

IV.1 ON FILIPPO TOMMASO MARINETTI   141
IV.2 THE FUTURIST DEBATE ON JOURNALS   147

CLOSING REMARKS:
THE ARTISTIC ACTION AS SOCIAL CRITIQUE   157

BIBLIOGRAPHY   165

FRANCO FERRAROTTI

FOREWORD

Art and society never confront one another. They are inside one another. Neither aesthetics as a "mirror" nor the notion of the aesthetic act as an exercising of the universally concrete do justice to the complexity of this embrace. Scholastic elaborations of ingenuous historical materialism, i.e. free from dialectic interaction, are not worth discussing, since their mechanistic nature is so evident. A society without artists, ignored because they are "non-productive" according to market forces, or one with its artists in prison or confined to psychiatric hospitals as asocial persons, runs the risk of imploding, or, at best, of stasis and stagnation; it loses the sense of direction in its evolution, its ability to foresee possible development beyond sheer actuality; it drowns in the eternal return of the identical, in the stifling passage from the same to the same.

Ilaria Riccioni's research clarifies that Surrealism was no escapism, but if anything, a hyper-reality; it led to the idea of a heightened reality. Futurism was logically an unprotected opening up to experimentation on brand-new unimagined potential. Its ambiguity was congenital: it exalted the myth of the roaring car while rejecting its coercive discipline, the structure of dominion linked to working to the clock. The nationalistic and therefore Fascist deviation was not necessarily the outcome. The essay by James Joll (*F.T. Marinetti: Futurism and Fascism*, in *Three Intellectuals in Politics*, Harper and Row, New York, 1960, pp. 131-184) was rather misleading on the topic since it took what it would like to prove as an indisputable presupposition. Like Ezra Pound, André Gide and other minor figures, also Gottfried Benn greeted Futurism with an arguably excessive enthusiasm: "The event that marked the foundation of modern art in Europe was the issuing of Marinetti's Manifesto of Futurism, which appeared on 20 February 1909 in Paris in *Le Figaro*. '*Nous allons assister à la naissance du Centaure*' – 'We're about to see the Centaur's birth,' he wrote, and: '…a roaring car [...] is more beautiful than the Victory of Samothrace.' These were the avant-gardists; individually however, they were already the realizers." (G. Benn, *Lo smalto sul nulla*, Adelphi, Milan, 1992, p. 270).

Benn's sensitive ear caught the short circuit between the avant-gardists and the realizers, the dialectic that eroded the link between the project and its implementation, perhaps the logical precipitation which, more than anticipating, mystified. In *La tentazione dell'oblio* (Laterza, Bari, 1993) I brought out the politically negative effects of these non-existent mediations, however, I also believe that I demonstrated that an authentic writer or artist, not a mere *écrivant* but an *écrivain*, to use the dichotomy of Barthes and Sartre to the degree in which it forces open the prison of current language, is by nature subversive, whatever his or her explicit political position, or name, Pound, Céline, Joyce or again Marinetti or Brodski. These were the diviners of technically progressive societies. They never let us forget that formal bureaucratic perfection was merely instrumental, not a final value. Surrealists and Futurists were not, as common opinion would have it, simplistically agreeable propagandists of "random words" in a sort of irresponsible fête of thought. In reality, they were the over-extenders of the language. From being Cartesian, clear and distinct, they tended to become emotional, heated, omni-embracing as an image, denying a logical-formal interpretation and with it the traditional punctuation mark, in fact freeing themselves from grammatical and syntactical constraints, to achieve pure music, to provoke the irreversible crisis of the myth of a two-chamber conception of the mind and joining the right and left hemispheres back together, as occurs paradigmatically in *Finnegan's Wake*.

The lack of awareness of those who have contrasted, with the spirit of a narrow shopkeeper's philistinism, the humanistic tradition and scientific research, as happened in the '60s with a British writer, a mediocre novelist but an efficient administrator (C.P. Snow, *The Two Cultures and the Scientific Revolution*) is so pathetic it is almost moving. This is not about reading Shakespeare to engineers or explaining the second law of thermodynamics to men of letters. More modestly, we must understand the emerging sensibilities, arguably no longer dogmatically catalogable, multiple, itinerant – instructive echoes and at the same time significant symptoms, signals and omens of society that are constantly renewed. It is in the attempt to grasp these cryptic messages and auroral forebodings that the praiseworthy intention of this research lies.

INTRODUCTION
TO THE NEW ENGLISH VERSION

This book is the result of a long-lasting research published 16 years ago in Italian.

The reception of this book was quite diversified at the time. For many reasons, avant-garde art was not considered to be a possible subject for a sociological study, so its fortune had been linked to a double resistance: the sociological community resistance and the historian of arts lack of interest. However, other typologies of readers were intrigued by this book: open minded scholars, designers, journalists with cultural tendencies, historians and any type of figure within the artistic network. Needless to say, that this work has been going on since then with the wider expectation to sociologically set evidences of how arts is a social phenomenon which is extremely necessary to our contemporary neoliberal society. The reason to re-publish it in English is a multiple one, on the one hand is motivated by research activity which is more and more International and, on the other hand, it is motivated in the very period of time we are experiencing, in Europe, but also in the US, in terms of forms of participation, forms of loss of democracy, forms of diffused irrational behaviours.

Marinetti's avant-garde of Futurism can be summed up as the ability to connect the social situations he observed through artistic activity; a utopia that could change the world not with new structures as alternatives to the preceding ones, but by destroying them and returning to the individual freedom of experimentation, a flexibility of expression at times without any practical use.

In the dialectic between man and machine, the Futurists saw a liberating dynamic for the evolution of sensibility. In relation to the machine, art could learn the new language of modernity and, through this language, communicate the changed difficulties of adaptation of the individual through new tools.

What is this art expressing at the beginning of a century which will turn out to be the century of Crime, totalitarianism and liberalism? Badiou, inquiring the Twentieth century and its peculiar irrationality, locate the core of his philosophical method in the answer to a crucial question: "what was thought in the century that was previously unthought?" (Badiou, 2005: 1-2); likely, in analysing art expression as a sort of history of sensitivity in social change, for that same century, I would turn the question into a sociological inquiry: *what was experienced in that century that was previously unexperienced?*

So, there are at least four crucial issues in the paradoxical trajectory of Futurism that can give us evidences of such *experience*: Art as a new social actor therefore avant-garde poses itself within the domain of critical thinking; Anticipation over its own time and space over future shapes of social conditions; A social act that in the present shapes artworks, apparently an individual action, but, *a posteriori* acts as a social action contributing to modify the threshold of perception, of taste and categories of imagination.

So the issue which is leading the book is that Futurism, more than other avant-gardes, was a "mentality", an attitude, a way of thinking the present with a prompt consequence in the behavior. The futurist political choices are embedded in such a complexity that is not possible to simply address it as Fascist Art. This connection is an easy escape but tends to trivialize a much more complex and differentiated reality within the movement, but also in the different phases of the futuristic parabola. Futurism was a revolutionary approach to every issue of everyday life as well as culture, history, religion. All social values were challenged through the double work of Manifestos and artworks. And the movement itself seem to be winking at both theorization of Adorno, on one hand, according to whom within the *isms* activity, as he calls it, "the essence of the provocation may be sought in the preponderance of art over artwork. (…) impulses of an art that transcends itself. *Isms* are potentially schools that replace traditional and institutional authority with an objective authority"(Adorno, 1997: 25) so destroying the idea of art as artworks; but, on the other hand, avant-gardes respond also to the need of a society to find new ways of expression in order to re-elaborate the history as such becoming a way to transformation: "a work of art can be called revolutionary if, by virtue of the aesthetic transformation, it represents, in the exemplary fate of individuals, the prevailing un-freedom and the rebelling forces, thus breaking through the mystified (and petrified) social reality, and opening the horizon of change (liberation)" (Marcuse, 1978: Introduction xi).

However, despite early twentieth century avant-garde art has been a widespread phenomenon with a number of different radical expressions within a couple of decades, they cannot be seen as one.

German Expressionism was pervaded by catastrophic elements, dominated by apocalyptic visions, strong contrasts, and essential figures; Rayonnism was strongly influenced and linked with all the most recent scientific studies over vibrations and lasted a very short span of time. Dada was the radical negation of reality, Surrealism a search for an over-reality. Futurism sprang from an optimistic expectation, like the Vorticism of Wyndham Lewis, but with a far more romantic view on the forthcoming development of the industrial era.

Futurism announced a momentous change that should impact not only the arts, but the whole of society, its morals, customs, even its most private and daily manifestations; however, this change was not an end but a beginning. What the Futurists announced was not a world that was sinking, but a world that was rising through a progressive chance offered by the changed conditions of life and opportunities opened by technology. They saw in the end of the past the beginning of a new era, and anticipated the possible social issues through new combinations of social power and structural organization. Furthermore, avant-garde was a critique of modernity but also a reaction to the "total" rationalization of society and, according to Simmel, a phenomenon deeply embedded in its own social conditions: *"Avant-garde is the evidence not only of radical thinking, but also lust for life, and it seems to appear whenever life has stopped to nourish the organized social structure"*. (Simmel, 1976: 126). Do we have contemporary expressions of avant-garde? Which shape is it assuming? Is it still in the art the domain of avant-garde, or has it shifted in other areas?

San Antonio, Texas, USA
February 20th, 2019

INTRODUCTION
FUTURISM: ANTICIPATING A NEW SOCIAL ACTION

This work originated in a search for signifieds. Certain sociological themes no longer studied seemed to me closer to the core of a living social issue, they left a production that was vast but at the same time mum with respect to the hardships and inconsistencies of contemporary phenomena. Sociology inquires the relational fabric of society, and it cannot, therefore, ignore the change of values and attitude in these relationships. What happened to the social context in the early decades of the twentieth century? How was that wave of violence over the relationship of the social actor with the environment reflected, over confidence in the outside world and the perception of being able to affect it? What exactly were the historical avant-garde movements? The symptom of a need to change, or merely a revolt going nowhere? It was necessary to enter a thorny contradictory framework devoid of living witnesses to interview. The task of the sociologist fused into that of the historian. What was Futurism? What did it say in its way of making art in that socio-historical period? Interpretation of this movement has remained half-finished, in the common opinion, lying somewhere between contemporary art, by definition incomprehensible, the provocative and arrogant attitude of a small group, and a reaction against a historical moment that violently accelerated everyday life. In this study, I have tried to provide the opportunity to check those words that were deemed the spearhead of a generational change.

I have certainly used some concepts of the sociology of knowledge, but substantially, I have interpreted this movement from a sociological perspective paying attention to its deeply ambiguous and contradictory nature in order to understand at which condition can avant-garde originate.

Precisely in view of its fragmentary nature, and the richness and ambiguity of the phenomenon, I have tried to form some potential conceptual categories, and it will ultimately be up to the reader to decide whether they alone can contain the sense I sought to give them.

I have chosen a "participant" position, starting, therefore, from that criterion for which there is no dissociability between the object and the method of investigation, both of which appear of equal importance for the purposes of accumulating knowledge[1].

Any scientific inquiry needs a model to structure a logical path, albeit temporarily, through which to establish a relationship of sense between abstract conceptual entities and empirical data. In this study, I have not used a model in the proper sense, but I have used some conceptual categories to guide the observations. In this case, the empirical data are documents. The model consists in a trace of the significant moments of the movement's constitution and self-representation, comparing these with some socio-critical theories.

During my observations, I have allowed the logic of the movement's artistic developments to emerge, where by "logic" is meant a pivot that summarizes and integrates:

1) action with the sense of achieving an objective;

2) the unintended peripheral consequences that the presence of this movement stimulated in society;

3) the historical reasons and cultural events that generated this artistic reaction.

From this point of view, Futurism would seem to have opened the way to a new sociological category: an artistic endeavour that initially presented itself as a reaction, but at the same time had a sense of achieving an objective, therefore "Social Action" to all intents and purposes, which, on an individual front, was active in the processing and refining of human and relational qualities, as well as aiming at social emancipation.

In the past, R. Arnheim, in *Art and Visual Perception* (Berkley, 1954), one of the first studies to relate the study of art to Gestalt psychology, recognized the study of artistic phenomena as an integral part of the study of mankind. For Arnheim, the contemporary individual tends to neglect the gift of understanding through the senses, and for this same reason, concepts are separated from perception and thought becomes abstract[2]. We can clearly deduce that the author considers sensory perceptions the root of thought, the triggering element, the motive behind any search and processing, be it intellectual or artistic.

---

1   Franco Ferrarotti, *Trattato di sociologia* (Turin: UTET, 1968), II ed., p. 288.
2   Rudolph Arnheim, *Arte e Percezione Visiva* (Milan: Feltrinelli, 1962), p. 2.

"That a whole cannot be attained by the accretion of isolated parts was not something the artist had to be told. For centuries, scientists had been able to say valuable things about reality by describing networks of mechanical relations; but at no time could a work of art have been made or understood by a mind unable to conceive the integrated structure of a whole"[3].

Futurism proposed to give vent to creativity as a historical human quality and not a supernatural one, and beginning from this assumption, its every noisy manifestation assumed the substance of an invitation for the common individual to become a sharer in the exercising of this quality. Marinetti's objective was that of a "new world" in which to live free from traditional social constraints in a multicultural and cosmopolitan context. From this perspective, the artistic movement of Futurism arose as a simultaneous symptom of and cure for the crisis in Western culture, and in this sense, a sociological study of the phenomenon becomes necessary to observe the social context in the early twentieth century, but especially what that context managed to generate that was prophetic in respect to the present century.

From the artistic-creative explosion of all the avant-garde movements of that period we can study the evolution of contemporary social relations and operations, passing via social constriction and the progressive standardization of the society in which we live.

Artistic skill means knowing how to balance things through a creative effort aimed at transforming reality, and the capacity to be a part of society but also to stand outside it. From here arises the misunderstanding of so much culture in retrospect that sees a human reality in the "multiplicity" of identities so widely exalted also by Futurism. This is to be reappraised as a creative quality that slots into a context of transcending and transforming reality, thereby acquiring dignity of action.

There are different degrees of reality: the available world and art benefit from different degrees of reality, but this does not mean that the degree of reality of the phenomenal world has a greater substance than that of art.

One study which partially incorporates some of Arnheim's concepts still places the artistic issue in its relationship with reality: "Artists and their exploiters place themselves on a privileged plane with respect to that of the everyday world since they possess an important possibility which is

---

3   *Ibid.*, p. XX.

excluded in 'normal' experience: that of being able to check the material reality of the experience that they wish to give birth to"[4].

Artistic reality is multidimensional and therefore very close to reality as an experience, and in this sense, art sinks its roots in the sensory world and communicates in the form of works, of communicative labour transformed into matter. In the artistic corpus there therefore exists a knowledge of reality that travels different roads from science, but that shares the desire for knowledge and detail in its methodological tools.

Perhaps we cannot speak of a greater degree of reality in either of the two cognitive processes; the scientific and the artistic are mutually different but somehow interpenetrate, and often reach similar conclusions.

I shall be following the logic of action of the artistic movement as a guiding thread of the social action it brought to life. The first conceptual category is that of the avant-garde. Which already contains the concept of *social role*.

Sometimes the explanation of a phenomenon can have an irreproachable logical coherence and a factual background, but may be completely lacking in intention, since, instead of studying the outside, it may yield to the temptation of a conceptual reproduction of itself, with the inevitable condemnation to a routine work that explains nothing except its own internal coherence.

By observing artistic reality in the light of the findings of Gestalt theory, Arnheim took the ground that unites this psychology with artistic perception, supported by the fact that much research set out to show that "the appearance of any part depends, to a greater or lesser extent, on the structure of the whole"[5].

The impulse that unites these cognitive processes seems to be that of the search for unity, each perception is also *thought*, each reasoning is also *intuition*, and each observation is also *invention*. Consequently, visual perception becomes a creative way to grasp reality, but these processes are typical of all mental activities: "Just as the prosaic search for information is 'artistic' because it involves giving and finding shape and meaning, so the artist's conceiving is an instrument of life, a refined way of understanding who and where we are"[6].

---

4   Marco Sambin, *Arte e percezione visiva. Indicazioni per una metodologia nell'analisi del grado di realtà in arte*, in L. Pizzo Russo (ed.), "Estetica e Psicologia", (Bologna: il Mulino, 1982), pp. 138-139.
5   Rudolph Arnheim, *op. cit.*, p. XX.
6   *Ibid.*, p. XXI.

So long as experience was considered an indistinct agglomerate of stimuli, it was possible to manipulate it arbitrarily, visual perception was a subjective imposition of reality and its forms:

> In fact, no student of the arts would deny that individual artists or cultures form the world after their own image. [...] This objective element in experience justifies attempts to distinguish between adequate and inadequate conceptions of reality. Furthermore, all adequate conceptions might be expected to contain a common core of truth, which would make the art of all times and all places potentially relevant to all men. [...] a badly needed antidote to the nightmare of unbounded subjectivism and relativism.
>
> Finally, there was a wholesome lesson in the discovery that vision is not a mechanical recording of elements but rather the apprehension of significant structural patterns. [...] In other words, here was a scientific analogy to the fact that images of reality can be valid even though far removed from a 'realistic' semblance.[7]

According to these studies, which remain, albeit dated, *the* reference point for an observation of visual perception applied to artworks, artistic production is, together with scientific production, the place where the unity of thought and the perception of reality can be most easily recognized.

The artistic context is not only the domain of vision, but also of the word, of the organization of sense through language, of music. The formation of perception and measurement is continuously remodelled and put to the test by the communicative stimuli that each object, environment and situation impose on the sensibility of the individual inserted in an urban situation.

Perception, in turn, is merely the spark that excites the spaces of imagination which give life to artistic creation, and this imagination is not detached from the forces in action necessary to create, or from the imagery that past art provides as historical-existential baggage; but is in a dynamic relationship with both the social symbols crystallized from taste, and from those defined by the work of art itself.

Duvignaud spoke in this sense of *"enracinement de la création dans l'expérience collective"* as a condition of its existence. He confirmed the individual in relation to his or her environment and social context at the centre of these studies, and art, in turn, in relation to the expectations of an era, a group, an individual, and within the framework of the *"genre de société qui supposent des expériences chaque fois différentes de rapports humains, de sentiments et d'émotions, il faut donc, pour mesurer l'enracinement de*

---

7   *Ibid.*, p. XXI.

la création imaginaire, définir doublement cette dernière par rapport aux attitudes artistiques conscientes ou implicites, et par rapport à la fonction que l'art exerce dans un type particulier de société"[8], at which point we can review the different aesthetic attitudes and diversity of roles that the various imaginary creations assume depending on social structures.

It is presumed that avant-garde art launched a conception of art as a source of communication, a kind of art that operated in the historical context as much as it was generated by it, thus using artistic expressiveness as a type of communication that explained current relations between the subject's interior world and the external one of production and socializing. We can often speak of artistic action having an anticipatory property regarding the tendential guidelines of taste and cultural needs that will affect other layers of production.

Art can be revealed as a tool that helps observe the social link of expressiveness with institutions, culture and social changes that are in continuous evolution: abstraction as an echo of social immateriality, for example.

Artistic fortune is linked to many contingent variables. Art is the "undefined" part of society, its living part, what Adorno and Horkheimer defined "the unconscious historiography of society"[9]. Its structures are the organization and the obstacle to the transfiguration of society in community, but also a guarantee with respect to organizing the system. Change is a summary of the dialectic between these two components.

Thus, reality is constructed by culture, society, and the individuals who observe and make it; art is a way of seeing this reality, is an act that draws inspiration from it but absolutely does not represent a "photocopy" of it. Because of this, the real link to be deciphered concerns the relationship between the artistic object and reality. There can be no talk of arbitrariness in an artistic interpretation of the world, nor of recognizable laws; perhaps it is more appropriate to think of art as *allusion*.

Contemporary art arose as a rupture, the first being the avant-garde works. Horkheimer argued that in their aesthetic behaviour people are "stripped" of their social functionality and react as individuals, consequently, the antisocial moment of modern art has a very precise sense: a cornerstone

---

8   J. Duvignaud, *Sociologie de l'Art*, Paris, PUF, 1967, pp. 52-53.
9   Max Horkheimer, Theodor W. Adorno, *Lezioni di Sociologia* (Turin: Einaudi, 1966-2001), p. 117.

of the scandal of current society causes the wrath of "normality" which, through its very reaction, reveals a profound falsehood[10].

If Horkheimer's idea is true that, "to speak of culture was always contrary to culture", it is also true that Futurism, and avant-garde art in the broadest sense, used art as a means of appropriating reality rather than for a detached analysis. This artistic movement "proposed" a vision of reality, while critical sociology arrived at a philosophical reflection by observing the social process in its becoming.

However, that of the Institute of Social Research in Frankfurt is a far-sighted critique about the spectacular trend of contemporary society: with art alone it cannot escape from the utilitarian calculation that the whole of capitalist society depends on, we can however make an attempt, open a gap dictated by a utopia, by the gesture released from the necessity of calculation, thereby indicating the possibility of a transcendence of the concrete datum, and especially that it averts the exhaustion of the individual and of society itself in its economic-productive functionality. And it is precisely in this perspective that we can interpret the trend that is expressive of the avant-garde and its research.

Art relates the visible to the invisible, is a "detonator of sense" which, if it does not provide concrete reality, does prompt us to connect the facts through new links[11]. But if individuals and their mode of movement in society were historical realities for Horkheimer, artistic transfiguration could not be strongly linked to the context of birth and development in which an artistic trend is to operate. The very need for sustained momentum hyperbolically projected into a future art, falls into a context of social crisis, a deep rift between the past and the present in which the avant-garde movements seemed to have taken the role of artistic entertainers for a future that had not yet been glimpsed but was hopefully on its way.

The future outlined was predominantly technological. The charm of speed brought with it that of simultaneity: the discovery that in different points of the earth the same thing was happening at the same time, this universalism that technology revealed to mankind, may have been the true origin of the new conception of time and the occasional discontinuous traits with which modern art depicted life[12].

---

10 *Ibid.*, p. 117.
11 Remo Bodei, conference, "Teseco per l'Arte", 22.02.2001, Pisa.
12 Arnold Hauser, *Storia sociale dell'arte*, vol. IV, Turin, 1955-56, pp. 373-374 in M. Horkheimer, T.W. Adorno, *op. cit.*, p. 119.

Social organization conceived as an extended community, might perhaps leave room for the creation of shared values, also starting from their aesthetic fickleness. Enter the immateriality of relationships. These first modernist artists and thinkers seem to have adopted a way to enter both reality and the back story, details that could reveal the nuclei of the rupture and discomfort which, with greater responsibility, launched processes of change in both contemporary culture and individuals.

CHAPTER I
THE SOCIAL ROLE OF ART:
RELATIONS AND INTERTWINIGS IN ART AND
SOCIETY

I.1 *The Breakdown Implicit in the Arrival of Industrial Society*

I.1.a *The Concept of Avant-garde Art*

Erwin Panofsky observed that it is practically impossible to scientifically determine when an object becomes a work of art, in other words when form takes precedence over function:

"When I write to a friend to invite him to dinner, my letter is above all a tool of communication; but the more attention I pay to the form of my writing the more it tends to become a work of calligraphy; the more attention I pay to the form of how I express myself, the more it tends to become a literary and poetic work"[1].

It seems that this is precisely the game of the avant-garde, namely, creating art and then defining it as such in order to root their identity only in their own production.

An another note, Arnold Hauser detected in the relationship between the renewal of artistic forms and the resistance of the current style of an era, the fundamental figure of the public, who almost always determine a change in aesthetic habits before the institutions and critics do.

"As a rule, to shake a deeply-rooted artistic production and cause a radical change in taste, we need the appearance of a new public"[2] writes Hauser

Other drivers of artistic change seem to derive from multiple interconnected sources such as the birth of a new public, political transformations, and the pressure of the profession[3], from whose structural

---

1   Cfr. Erwin Panofsky, *Meaning in the Visual Arts. Papers in and on Art History* (New York: Anchor Books, 1955) p. 14.
2   Arnold Hauser, ibid., p. 31.
3   Vera L. Zolberg, *Constructing a Sociology of the Arts* (Cambridge: Cambridge University Press, 1990), p. 165.

features is freed the power to promote or impede the access of artworks as a triggering factor of change.

The more art works are visible and public, the more their influence on taste and aesthetics can easily enter a dialectical relationship with the outside world, joining the twofold relationship of a taste modifier and modified.

In Poggioli's interpretation, the concept of avant-garde art was born with the historical awareness of the artist as an observer and interpreter of reality and history. However, we cannot define it as *avant-garde* before this concept was knowingly born.

According to Antoine Compagnon, the avant-garde movements were imposed on early modern artists because of the substantial diversity of their approach at that time: the avant-garde movements would forestall the fate of obsolescence by becoming historical, "Presenting the movement of the new as a critical overcoming"[4]. Warding off obsolescence since they relied for their artistic effectiveness not only on aesthetics as an artistic transformation in a dialectic with the real, but also and above all because the avant-garde became art in the service of its time.

For example, Futurism entered society precisely because it made itself an instrument of contemporaneity, used modern communication techniques, and presented itself aesthetically as avant-garde from an expressive point of view. Plus, it managed to express the present with images of the future, tackling the dialectic of creation by exploiting

> the principle according to which the dialectic of artistic creation is expressed in a more unique and more intense way in reciprocal dependence of the contents and forms of expression, of the reasons and means, of artistic vision and technique, which therefore means, in essence, that the experience to configure and the idea to communicate are not already beautiful and ready before their means of expression become available. The artist knows what he has to say only when he already knows how he will say it.[5]

The term 'avant-garde art' was born from Marinetti's insights into the world to come, on prophecies dictated by a scientific renewal, the change in the perception of space-time, and the relationship of the individual to the new reality. Marinetti was the only one who really fully married the logic of this race for the future, proclaiming "futility and transience" as the fundamental character of this new art since he "above his followers had the gift of

---

4   Antoine Compagnon, *I cinque paradossi della modernità* (Bologna: il Mulino, 1993), p. 42.

5   Arnold Hauser, *Sociologia dell'arte*, vol. II, (Turin: Einaudi, 1977), p. 76.

SALE
325   4 1680710   12/01/2022   16:59

Today you were served by WENDY

FUTURISM
9788869772313   1x   15.00   15.00
DISCOUNT   75.00%   15.00   11.25-
                                  ....
TOTAL   ITEMS   1   3.75
                                  ....
Offline card   £3.75

VAT INCLUDED IN ABOVE TOTAL AMOUNT

RATE   0.00%   0.00   IN   3.75

THANK YOU FOR SHOPPING AT BLACKWELL'S

www.Blackwells.co.uk

CHOOSE FROM OVER 15 MILLION BOOKS ONLINE
RESERVE ONLINE, COLLECT INSTORE
FREE UK delivery on ALL orders

REFUND POLICY

We want you to be happy with everything you
buy at Blackwell's. However, if you are not
satisfied with your purchase please return
it in person within 30 days with your receipt.

BLACKWELL UK LTD
Registered in England No. 796591
50 Broad Street, Oxford OX1 3BQ
VAT Number 532 5855 39

prophecy. And not because he was really a prophet but because he intuited a point of crucial depth: the changes that science and technology as well as industrialism and new forms of communication would bring to the field of creativity and art"[6]. Avant-garde became a broad concept, which defined a way of looking at the interconnections between art and reality, between art and society; rather than an artistic trend, the avant-garde assumed the characteristics of a "behaviour", a new attitude towards reality.

It was about *how* to think of art and not *what* a thought or an artistic work was; it was about inventing, in the urgency of social transformations, a way that was "totally revolutionary to look at creative phenomena even in their 'total' interconnection, whose consequences Marinetti was certainly the first to assess, across the board, even at the extremes"[7].

What was this new conception of the avant-garde nourished by, if not by the unprotected violent projection towards an invented future?

Returning to the origins of the inventor of the movement's literary passion, we can see one passage as fundamental as it is neglected of the nature of his literary style and inventiveness: his Symbolist past. By the term 'Symbolist past' it is not intended here so much a love for Symbolist literature, but an artistic vein that arose as an antecedent basis for his subsequent creative adventures (in all senses).

Marinetti wrote and published in French some poems and tragedies, before the proclamation of the Manifesto in 1909: such as the drama *Paul Baglione*, inspired by Victor Hugo, which remained unpublished; shortly afterwards he approached French symbolism obtaining assignments at the *Revue d'Art Dramatique,* the most prestigious theatrical magazine of the end of the century. Through his writings on theatre published as a correspondent, can be discerned the developing ideas that would become the generators of the Futurist avant-garde: "The refusal of bourgeois ethics, the inclination toward a strong scenically meaningful drama, the freedom of the artist against the traditional rules of art, the heroic tension towards the ideal, contempt for naturalistic *Verismo*, an interest in the scenic vitality of dramatic action, an opting for the irreverent values of the grotesque and ironic"[8].

In this sense, so many criticisms of Futurism as a movement without memory become negligible in the light of a memory of a different type, an unconscious memory which Marinetti drew on through a reading of the

---

6   Maurizio Calvesi, *Marinetti, inventore dell'avanguardia,* in "Marinetti e il Futurismo", Catalogue (Rome: De Luca, 1994), p. 1.
7   *Ibid.*, p. 1.
8   Giovanni Lista, *Marinetti tra simbolismo e Futurismo,* in "Primafila" a monthly periodical on theatre and live performance, no. 7, May 1995, pp. 43-44.

sacred texts of Hinduism and Buddhism[9], criticizing Symbolist idealism, but sparing its imaginative and transforming power.

I.1.b *The Escape from History*

The beginning of the twentieth century was defined in sociology with Weber's study of "Typologies": social action, the individual, society, all the components of human living and action could be observed and made scientifically significant through classification by type. The type helped the assimilation of similarity in a historical context whose dominant social motive was the birth of the masses as a new "unit of social measure".

The scientific need became that of being able to provide broad coordinates in observing the movements of this mass. Weber's Ideal Type brought "meaning to meaningless infinity", contextualized, cropped a part of the real to shed light on portions of a reality that had been discovered as much more complex than in the pre-industrial era.

The progressive social transformation caused by the industrial revolution was present in its most official and concrete guise in France and Germany. The French workers' movement was already stirring by the end of 1850, and the Germans spontaneously followed it a dozen years later; the motivations being to safeguard the rights of factory work, and encourage workers' political awareness. In Leipzig, the German Workers' Association movement was founded under the leadership of Ferdinand Lassalle which sought to increase awareness among the working class of the conquest of universal suffrage, which could be followed up by prospective recognition and support for the independent cooperatives of producers.

The national unions were born: first that of the German tobacco workers, then the printers' union in 1866, and in 1868 that of the tailors and woodworkers.

In the meantime, in France after the Paris Commune, the workers' movement reached a considerable strength, the first congress of workers, which met in 1874, establishing an inspectorate for the first time, ensuring legislative protection of work[10].

In these countries, there was already a steady awareness of the conditions and rights of workers at the end of the nineteenth century, which was

---

9   *Ibid.*, p. 48.
10   Valerio Castronovo (ed.), *Storia Economica Cambridge*, vol. 8*, (Turin: Einaudi, 1992), pp. 646-667.

indicative of the battles and partial compromises that had needed tackling in previous years.

In Italy, the situation was lagging, industry was present but with small factories that were above all manufacturing and agricultural, and mainly located in Milan, Turin, Genoa and Naples.

"In 1861, the machine industry was concentrated above all in Genoa and Naples. A ballpark census of Italian workshops at the time of the Paris Exhibition in 1867 listed seventy factories with about 9,000 workers, now the number of workshops of some importance should be increased to around 150, with 15 thousand workers and an annual production worth 35 to 40 million. There are currently at least 8 or 10 factories in which the production value exceeds one million, and more than one in which it reaches or surpasses double this figure"[11].

The machine industry was growing, but in its structural and social conditions, Italian industrialization was in a very different situation from France and Germany. The attempt was to bring unity and a sense of solidarity with the masses through trade unions while trying to find points in common between the classes. The governments needed to create great myths where an indefinite number of individuals could see a part of themselves reflected and protected in the new order that created more and more distance from the institutions.

With the obligatory exclusion of the masses by the State, the Unification of Italy had in some way sealed the authority and power of the free state. The national will exhibited to the government actually conformed only to that part of the bourgeoisie connected to the ruling class.

It seemed only the presence of the masses could bring about substantial changes in social organization. The protagonist on the horizon of the new century was "the crowd", as found in no end of late nineteenth-century and early twentieth-century literature: Charles Baudelaire, Edgar Allan Poe, Scipio Sighele, and Gustave Le Bon. Essentially, the approach of poets, artists and scholars was a rejection of the indistinct wretchedness of "the masses" as a situation of normality.

In sociological analyses, the theoretical constructions most relevant of the early twentieth century were, in Italy, those of Pareto, Mosca, and Michels. The elite theorists. We can see in Pareto's theory a substantial "negative" consideration of irrational aspects of societal change. Having structured his sociological theory according to a uniform scheme of society inherited from Comte, Pareto developed a social theory of its historical

---

11   Giuseppe Colombo, *Industria e politica nella storia d'Italia* (Bari-Rome: Laterza, 1985), pp. 241 and 245.

context dictated in part by a disillusioned vision of science and of the distance between reality and theory.

Elitism seems to have arisen partly from a protection of intellectual activity as a search for truth, which, to remain such, must safeguard its processing by withdrawing and remaining at the disposal of the chosen few.

Futurism seemed partially to want to be reborn from the pessimism inherited from the previous epoch, going against the reality that the social scientists wanted to investigate, but not without some frustrating consequences.

> Behind the disenchanted expressions of Pareto's realism, one clearly sees the basic pessimism of the second half of the century in which faith in the automatic progress of the human species and the enlightenment promises of a triumphant, universal rationality, seemed wholly shipwrecked and betrayed. In Pareto, this pessimism is openly transformed into a bitter mockery of democratic and humanitarian ideals, seen as illusory, whilst in Weber and Durkheim, his two great contemporaries, it emerges with the deep, provocative pathos which accompanied the proletarianization of the spirit and the painful nostalgia for an organically combined humanity, dominated not by individual hedonistic caprice, but the ethical imperatives of the great social institutions.[12]

In 1916, Pareto published the *Treatise on General Sociology* in which he identified human nature and social consequence, mainly oriented from irrationality. In it he would come to say that society was moved more by non-logical actions than logical ones.

One important distinction that Pareto made in presenting his social theories was in respect to the different angles from which such theories can be interpreted, from the point of view of their truth or falsity, or their persuasive force and social usefulness.

Although his treatise is substantially chaotic, full of digressions, and draws also on a comparison of Roman and Greek cultures, it does have the merit of making headway in an impenetrable topic, seldom dealt with.

On the other hand, he certainly deserved much of the criticism he encountered among scholars and social scientists: the statement that the subjective elements, which he calls "instincts", although they are not of objective existence and therefore change from person to person, always become a constant to consider in interpreting phenomena.

---

12   Franco Ferrarotti, *Vilfredo Pareto: the disenchanted world of conservative pessimism,* An International Review, vol. 6, no. 2, Spring 1986.

These instincts, giving rise, for everyone, to an intense mental activity that is used to explain the instinctive element through reason. The result is a figment of the imagination so variable that, if not considered in the formulation of sociological theories, is likely to create confusion between the results of imaginative work and events of concrete reality.

So, how can we find this continuous scrap, consisting of non-logical actions, and its explanation given by reasoning? Pareto avoids this impasse with an example on the different considerations we may have on the author of an action: either we consider the intention of the author and his psychic state, or we analyse what he said. In other words, either we believe in the intention, or we grant veracity to the correspondence between action and experience.

Pareto had already written an economics treatise, in which he presented the coordinates of a theory of economic equilibrium, and during these observations became aware of the real difficulty of finding a precise scientific interpretation of social phenomena. In the formulation of his sociological thinking, we find constant references to the "mind", "psychic states", "people", and "context" (all traits he considered founding of the social humus and the deep roots behind its motives), and through this terminology he entered a study of society via the individual and the psychic states that actions are based on.

On this basis, he developed a crucial distinction in social actions that deepens and explains more widely the rational action of Weber. Pareto made the distinction between logical and non-logical actions, observing how actions are actually driven by pre-existing reasons among social actors, such as language: "It is time to acquire a first concept of the nature of non-logical actions and their importance in social phenomena"[13].

These ways of considering social phenomena are, from a logical-experimental aspect, "lacking any precision and without any rigorous agreement with the facts, while we cannot deny the immense importance they have in history and in the determination of social equilibrium"[14].

However, this led to the need to reconsider the concept of "separation" that Pareto had made previously in his treatise, of the experimental truth of certain theories and their social usefulness; two aspects that are not only jumbled, but can also be, and often are, in contradiction.

---

13   Vilfredo Pareto, *Trattato di Sociologia Generale*, vol. II, (Milan: ed. Comunità, 1981), p. 1.
14   *Ibid.*, p. 2.

One of the major causes of the failure of certain social theories is, for the author, precisely the lack of awareness of this substantial difference between the study of a phenomenon as it should be and how it actually is. "We are fully within the field of logical-experimental science when instead of studying, for example, what a family must be, we study what it actually was"[15].

Note the use of the language, "The word, whether written, or solemnly expressed, appears to childlike peoples as something mysterious, and faith itself gives it a supernatural force. For the ancient Roman, the word was power; it bound and freed. If it fails to move mountains, it nevertheless has the power to move the harvest from one field to another, belonging to others; it is powerful enough to evoke the divinity and make them abandon the besieged city"[16].

He took this consideration from R. Ihering, *Esprit du droit romain*, however, Pareto acutely observed that the structure of Roman Law was based on associations between words and facts, leaving room to progress within the context of these associations.

The structure of the form and mechanism of ancient Roman Law, although leaving almost no free will to the parties and the magistrate, did leave room for progress, a progress based on an immutable psychic state given that it was fixed on associations between very precise words and forms, which resulted in an alternation of duplicities.

And it was here that Pareto saw the futility of certain logical motives entrusted to actions, since, not being covered by the verbal scheme, they can find no room in social reality. They act in the form of unrecognized actions, which he called "non-logical" and that, in their theoretical construction, constitute the magmatic, active and daily part of social action, and therefore also the potentially seditious part or the one responsible for change.

Further on in his treatise, Pareto examines the word '*religio*', by which he seems to indicate a state of mind, an attitude: "We shall limit ourselves to observing that even in the Classical era, one of the senses of '*religio*' was without doubt that of painstaking, scrupulous, diligent care. It is a state of mind that establishes certain constraints which are strongly imposed on the consciousness. So, if one wished to choose a term to express the psychic state we spoke of previously, the one that seems most suitable would be the term '*religio*'"[17].

---

15   *Ibid.*, p. 7.
16   Vilfredo Pareto, *Trattato di Sociologia Generale*, vol. I, (Milan: ed. Comunità, 1981), p. 152.
17   *Ibid.*, p. 159.

European culture between the nineteenth and twentieth centuries was therefore the scene of a battle on several fronts: the cultural hegemony of the Church being replaced by values such as science, progress, tolerance, and reason.

Industrialization had brought with it a gradual growth of secular states. The need for a "religious" mentality, scrupulous, meticulous and repetitive, which had led Pareto to identify a moral code based on a series of fictions, given that the Roman '*religio*', more than that of Athens, was particularly concerned with the exterior actions of worship, regardless of the intention, and transferred the need for discipline and order to scientific doctrines and the use of reason.

In this lay context, writes Sergio Romano: "Religion survives in the field of the opponent. Positivism and socialism were very often lived as 'religions of mankind' in which God and his saints were replaced on the altars of the new myths: progress, welfare, and education. There is more religion in Europe in the first half of the twentieth century, than there was in the second half of the previous century. But to the great annoyance of the Churches, this religion has adopted other idols and other objectives"[18].

Therefore, the study of Pareto on logical and non-logical actions was to separate élites value-loaden logical actions from non-logical actions mixed with emotions, complicities, instinctive decisions, and reasons of action not directly logical in the sense of economic loss-and-win kind of action.

In 1921, Marinetti published *The New Moral-Religion of Speed*:

> After dynamic art, the new moral religion of speed. [...] Christian morals served to develop the internal life of man. It no longer has any reason to exist today, since it has been emptied of everything Divine. Christian morals defended human physiology from the excesses of sensuality. Moderated its instincts and balanced them. Futurist morals will defend man from decomposition determined by slowness, memory, analysis, rest and habit. Human energy centuplicated by speed will dominate time and space.[19]

The century was characterized by a need for the new that sought to replace old patterns with fresh contexts and contents. In 1900, Pèguy founded *Cahiers de la Quinzaine*, bringing together Socialism, Christianity and Nationalism; in 1907 Bergson wrote *Creative Evolution*, in which the

---

18   Sergio Romano, *La cultura europea tra Otto e Novecento. Religione, Arte, Politica*, in "Nuova Storia Contemporanea", year V, no. 5, September, October 2001 (Florence: Le Lettere, 2001), pp. 5-6.

19   F.T. Marinetti, *Lussuria-Velocità*, Milan, Modernissima, 1921, p. 157.

themes of intuition and the *élan vital* were taken up and developed; Sorel wrote *Reflections on Violence* in 1906.

Freud's *Interpretation of Dreams* and *Formulations on the Two Principles of Mental Functioning* were published respectively in 1899 and 1911, through which room was made for a conception of reality as subjective perception, as a creation of the mind that filters the present in the light of the schemes of experience, with knowledge of the psyche opening the doors to the manipulation of reality.

The subjective dimension of reality had been discovered, which somehow added an important component to Pareto's understanding of logical and non-logical actions, in which it was believed possible to operate discernment only when subjectively perceived reality was separated from the objective kind.

A further and not secondary aspect of the sociology of the time, and of Pareto, was the observation of the elite: every clique of power was an elite, even the liberal state essentially confirmed that laws, customs, and the facts considered relevant belonged to the "psychic state" of elected representatives who determined them, while the masses were limited to accepting this situation.

In this sense, the study of the non-logical was the path indicated to study real social conditions which were not those dictated by the ruling classes, the elite, but those that did not correspond to "logical" patterns, since they were part of a different logic.

Pareto observed the splitting of the social context and divided the two realities which complied, that of the elite, which emptied itself of meaning despite being in power, and that of the masses with no powers in an institutional sense but which determined the real progress of social life. "Futurism fits into the climate of that new European nationalism which will present two contrasting, and in the long run irreconcilable faces: opening to the masses and the refoundation of the elite"[20].

At the same time, in 1907, the German Association of Craftsmen, *Deutscher Werkbund*, was founded in Munich, a free union of intellectuals, industrial, professionals, artists and craftsmen that set out to establish a link between industrial production and the "human" characteristics of work, between industrial activity and artistic production.

Mindful of the experience of the English Arts and Crafts movement and its followers, the *Werkbund* did not adopt positions that were too

---

20   Maurizio Serra, *Al di là della decadenza* (Bologna: il Mulino,1994), p. 23.

extreme either against the industrial process, nor in favour of creation on the artisan model.

The substantial critical point of the movement arose in respect of the lower quality and aesthetic content of the industrial product in the face of artistic aesthetic research, and, while not opposed to industrial production, it did criticize its overly apparent economic goals.

In 1914 Germany, Berlin was in the full-blown expressionist context, and another version of the revolt against the models of bourgeois culture could be seen, which did not end only in cultural subversion, however.

Also in this case, the artistic movement was the voice of a "human" need, a "spiritual" attitude, (meaning metaphysical, ethical, civil and only lastly, appearance), which married over the course of a prolonged period, several trends, ideologies and aesthetic forms that, in time, would constitute the movement's wealth.

In England, this was the period of Vorticist movement with EzraPound, Wyndham Lewis, and the members of the Rebel Art Centre. In 1914, the magazine *Blast* was published by Lewis, the Vorticist "manifesto", with a clear Futurist resonance, containing a series of institutions, personages and customs to be banished from culture.

Like Marinetti, Lewis also saw the crises of the turn of the century as a phase of renewal, not of decadence; he felt the same warlike rancour, the same refusal of social equilibria as Futurism, but did not share the same love and unconditional trust for the role of the machine as the protagonist of the future. He was fully aware of the possibility in Futurism of slipping from a focus on the use of the machine as a means of production, to the function of the machine as a means of social revolution.

Vorticism lacked the romantic vein that essentially guided many of Futurism's theoretical choices. The historical European context showed, therefore, a cultural and artistic tendency that featured a psychological attitude as well as a need for expression.

The purely irrational and reactive intent took place precisely in this inversion of the use of culture, in a broad sense, as well as art. Art no longer served to express but to impress, to change the perceptive coordinates, in a word, to change history even before being able to enter it. The ambiguous position of the avant-garde, all the movements, appeared more disruptive and dispersive (although the first official one, Futurism, had entered history with disputation).

The perceived inability to enter history in a significant way, the impossibility of quickly changing a course that was directed towards the annulment of expression in favour of a precision in technique and technology, acted on the human soul, in the artistic one which is a banner of it, with a counteraction that sought to make art the double of history, i.e., a safe and imaginary haven.

Art was making war against history, was contesting it trying to remove from history the primacy of reality, and in this way, began to write a different history. For this reason, Futurist action was violent, art became communication, and for the first time entered the war as interventionist, but did not cross its own threshold of the virtual-creative action that might prove cathartic but might not change reality, in the final analysis. It could however have power over awareness. The freedom of the individual was exposed to a double peril: economic proletarianization and proletarianization of the soul.

This was the first confirmation, which the scientific field was just starting to become aware of, that on its own, structure cannot constraint life, as Simmel had perceived with clarity and thoroughness. The second was that communication was intimately a *gamayun*[21] of war.

A prophetic sign, a condition that indicated the proximity of an event, or an indicator. It was also expected that communicating, clarifying some reality in shadow, might give rise to a settling, to a reconsideration of previous positions, by opening up the conflict.

Art itself, if it became an instrument of action outside the gratuity of the creative act, would end its own life. It spoke but said nothing, it was idle in a context of missing history. It produced no history because it had lost its singularity.

The awareness of the nationalist and bourgeois intellectuals that the masses would be the true protagonists of politics, resulted in a focus on the construction of myths to make manipulation of the masses simpler by replacing the void left by religion.

It was urgent to face the education of the masses as such, as the individual seemed to be disappearing: "The transformation of the proletariat into an organized and powerful mass, accomplished by Socialism, showed that it was possible to educate the soul with discipline, devotion to the leaders, the enthusiasm of a faith"[22].

---

21   Ernst Jünger, *op. cit.*, pp. 11-13. Jünger uses the example of this colourful bird from the far North, which, when it appears in the heavens, indicates an exceptionality of climate, i.e., when the Arctic winter becomes too rigid, the waxwing is forced to find a home in lower latitudes. In this sense, he becomes a "climate prophet".

22   Emilio Gentile, *Il mito dello stato nuovo dall'antigiolittismo al fascismo* (Bari-Rome: Laterza, 1982), p. 14.

Studies by Le Bon had revealed the decisive role that sentiment played among the masses for the success of a novelty: it operated with the same strength as a religious conviction. The masses could be moved only by a myth's power of suggestion. Sorel too observed the centrality of the presence of a myth to mobilize the masses. Marinetti shared with Sorel the ethical-aesthetic taste for a fight, convinced that only through struggle could progress be born. And the new myth to nourish the masses was the project to abandon the past.

With this in mind, Marinetti operated with manipulatory acumen: the masses could not imagine anything not already known, the myth must therefore be aimed rearward, it was impossible to envisage a journey towards the unknown in an explicit manner, the easiest way to hook the imaginary was to flee from the dissatisfying known.

Violence combined with speed, machines as tools to facilitate entering the new, the birth of the status symbol as the virtual achievement of a precarious emancipation must become the new myth of the masses, the possibility of being projected into a future that could become dynamic only through acts that claimed to be the same.

The role of intellectuals was compacted on the most urgent communication front: dialogue with the masses, intellectual commitment, could directly enter the social field through dissemination, political and social commitment, freed thus of its traditional decorative role that history apparently reserved for it.

In the light of history, the political commitment of the avant-garde intellectual was within a diffused rejection of history and a shipwreck was inevitable, as happened to the French Surrealists and the Communist system, as well as to Futurism under Fascism in Italy and to Expressionism in Germany.

In Italy, Futurist theory was used by the Fascist regime in a partial manner, purged of its categorically subversive energies. Futurism had in its draft a "new morality", sexual freedom, liberation from the family as a refuge from life, the liberation of the word and expression, but the encounter with Fascism, despite an initial agreement, could only prove a failure. For the simple fact that one was a political movement and the other artistic: the point of departure may have been the same, but the objective was the contrary, one tending to control of the country's energies, the other aimed at liberating impulses from social constraints.

The failure was written upstream in the blocked relationship between sexuality and nationalism, with the maintenance of traditional morality, strengthened by control of the means of production. Built by a deviation or insufficiency of bourgeois society, Fascism tried in turn to suppress any form of deviance, on behalf of a dual sexual-racial phobia.[23]

Futurism aimed to liberate creative potentialities as an innovative and revolutionary engine to be dumped into the social and political context, but subjecting it to the supremacy of art. Politics could not have the same objective.

On both sides, violence was the instrument of extreme action to operate a reversal of the trend, but while in politics it was expressed in the form of totalitarianism, in art it was exposed to enslavement by forces that steered it towards the evil of dictatorships.

The emancipation of art from the ecclesiastical and regal precept, instead of taking it towards real autonomy, led to a dependence on progress, with a new strength which was that of Totalitarianism.

Did the artistic avant-garde really play such a decisive role in the spread of violence in Western culture? In that case, there must also have been a cultural identification with the artistic and expressive principles of certain social strata:

> The programmatic points of Futurism have no future, they do not depart from the turbid pre-logical charm of the socio-biological, they are reduced to obscure instincts – more than pre-modern, meta-historical – of a wholly instinctual sub-society. [...] But Futurism is not only this. [...] Their influence, literary but also political, is wide and jagged but singularly penetrating, up to the 'expressive' behaviour of our own times.[24]

It is indisputable that the Futurist movement was a fomenter and worshipper of violence, "war as hygiene of the world" is a leitmotiv of Futurist statements; it is equally true however that in the history of violence it was always a reaction or contrast to the "diluted" violence of power and rationalization. However, "Violence, being instrumental by nature, is rational to the extent that it is effective in reaching the goal that must justify it. [...] Violence can remain rational only if it pursues short-term objectives"[25], but Marinetti's goal was of dimensions so vast that it could not be thought of as a victory to be achieved in the short term.

The attempt to reconstruct the mentality and reality of a nation could not secretly have the illusion of succeeding in a short time. The renunciation

---

23   Maurizio Serra, *La ferita della modernità* (Bologna: il Mulino, 1992), p. 16.
24   Franco Ferrarotti, *La tentazione dell'oblìo* (Bari-Rome: Laterza, 1998), pp. 65-67.
25   Hannah Arendt, *Sulla Violenza* (Parma: Guanda, 1996), p. 72.

of rationality was in fact planned through a search for hidden logic from evidence of the facts. But if violence is nothing more than another mantle of power, in Futurism the size of power was subject to the logic of art: unpredictable, distant, and spectacular.

To speak of the Futurist movement means first and foremost making a division between two possible points of observation: one a movement of political, cultural, and media action, and a second an artistic movement, which many artists joined, for convenience not detaching themselves from the Marinettian nucleus, but not fully sharing his social theories, either.

A further consideration must then be made regarding the dissemination and reception of Futurist culture: sprawling, evenly varied and chaotic in the descriptions and analysis of the movement.

A third key point is that there is not one single Futurism, but several Futurisms, differing in their expression and political inclinations: Italian Futurism, Spanish Futurism and Russian Futurism. All to do with a breach. Futurism was therefore a tension towards what did not yet exist, a tension towards change, the space of action and creation that the modern context wished to arrange in every single aspect.

The Futurist manifesto, stated Marinetti, was dictated "for a single immense phalanx of souls: that of the strong and that of the exploited"[26].

He himself came from a family of the cultured upper class, his father an esteemed lawyer, his mother was a school teacher of literature. Marinetti's inheritance lay almost totally in the hands of that restless youth who returned to Milan from Egypt with his family, completing his studies and his intellectual forays to the wealthy Paris of the early twentieth century.

Apart from this biographical note in the public domain, Marinetti distinguished himself for a revolutionary impetus amplified by his intellectual and cultural tensions. The problem for Marinetti was not played out on an economic level, but on a psychic, nervous plane: reality could be changed through art precisely because it was an expressive prolongation of the relationship between dominant and individual cultures, a negotiation between social interests and subjective meanings.

Romantic naivety, perhaps, or extraordinary far-sightedness in perceiving culture as a profound motive of social change.

The myth of progress as the utopia of a new era highlighted the expectations of a century that came out of the consolidated security of the nineteenth century but was travelling with a frightening acceleration towards stasis.

---

26   Emilio Gentile, *op. cit.*, p. 141.

The machine was becoming the double of the individual, who adopted speed and automatism as desirable characteristics, qualities which in fact represented an irrational distraction from a no longer manageable world,

> with the outbreak of the first world war the equilibrium of nineteenth-century Europe shattered. Thus began, under the eyes of all, the real resigned despair of modern man, the reservations, the loss in front of the "great transformation". There is a gloomy sense of entering a new historical phase of walking on uncharted ground, on a journey where there are fewer old reference points.[27]

Marinetti sensed the advance of bureaucratization as an enemy of imagination; he fought his battle, however there is no battle without an army. The army he had available consisted of poets and painters, while the one he hankered to join was the people of the exploited, the proletariat.

In truth, Marinetti was aware from the outset that this was no class war, but one of survival: for some, survival resided in the possibility of using the imagination to transform reality, for others it belonged to the more immediately concrete possibility of surviving on more day-to-day fronts.

> We live upon the airy heights of the gigantic human mountain and seek to pour forth our flooding emotions in a song that longs for the star. We are well aware of the noxious black fogs exhaling from the hell in which you live your tormented lives, because the same gigantic, brute force prevents us from flying to the empyrean, and touching the stars with our brows.

In substance, the situation was common for those who wished to live apart from power, or, better still, for those who had other purposes and expectations.

> We feel and we think with you – and our song, just for one moment forgets its impossible paradises, to fall into the rhythm of that infernal reality. Brothers, we are but a single army that has lost its way in the dark wood of the Universe [...] our enemy is one and the same...Clericalism, commercialism, moralism, academicism, pedantry, pacifism, mediocrity...
> Trade unionists all, whether of manual labour or the intellect, of art and life, destroyers and creators together, realistic or idealistic anarchists, heroes of all strengths and of all beauties, let us go forward dancing propelled by the same superhuman intoxication, toward the common apotheosis of the Future![28]

---

27   Franco Ferrarotti, *Macchina e Uomo nella società industriale* (Turin: ERI, 1970), p. 34.
28   Filippo Tommaso Marinetti, *op. cit.*, pp. 141-142.

And in this he succeeded. Artistic expression, after Futurism, changed, it gave in to experimentation and the wall of Mannerism gradually crumbled.

But the basic revolt seemed paradoxically to be precisely against modernity, or better, the difficulty in the face of the total change in the social scenario urged the artist to engage in the social fabric, perceived to be wider, to finally abandon the role of the poet. The new context created a kind of guilt, a wound that it seemed difficult to heal.

"The advent of technique will therefore be idolized or demonized, but rarely accepted for what it is: the condition of scientific development arising from capitalist accumulation, i.e. the only form of positive society created by the 20th century"[29]. The rupture of the avant-garde was therefore the place to discover the non-logical, the non-expected and the non-known.

The attempted escape of art from history had its roots in art's non-membership of the logical processes of society, the logical and positivistic links of "mature capitalism that leaves no room for the 'structure of sentiments'"[30], surrendering in the face of the emergence of the masses as an irrational subject overpowering the elitist organization of power.

Only the intellectual could possess the tools to mediate between the masses and power, only the artist could embody the growing popular dissatisfaction within the social structures; the breaking point was therefore the moment when the evidence exceeded any test aimed at confuting it.

Futurism acted as a theoretical, artistic, political, and social movement; it is not easy to slot it into any socially recognized box, it had no precedent, and is evidence of the new that was on the move, with all the contradictions and denials that historical processes employ in defence of traditions.

It was, therefore, a breaking point, not an end. The breaking away of art, of Futurism, Expressionism, Vorticism and Surrealism from their historical context, opened a wound in scruples, a refusal of paternal authority and cultural patricide, which were all expressions of a lyrical activism that helped the avant-garde movements to exit from history conceived as an inevitable process, and to set themselves up as conscious action.

The crisis of liberalism and nationalism were the heritage of World War I, a last-ditch effort to unify the masses through the myth of a joint action against a more immediate enemy. "We were entering a historical

---

29   Maurizio Serra, *op. cit.*, p. 14.
30   Franco Ferrarotti, *Per conoscere Pareto* (Milan: Mondadori, 1973), p. 10.

conspiracy in which it was a matter of life or death to be able to overcome the idea of the nation as a constitutive form of collective life"[31].

The artistic project of the European avant-garde was, with Futurism and Marinetti at its head, evidence of a prompt understanding of the role that intellectuals and men of imagination would have in the new political-institutional scenario.

Recognizing in Futurist dynamism and creativity a promptness in understanding reality already answered and overwhelmed many of the statements and accusations of violence that might be brought against Futurist action.

Even Marinetti's Internationalist impetus, while defending nationalism, should be read as the intuition of a collaboration and solidarity founded on cosmopolitanism, the desire to form an elite of lovers of the avant-garde, which would create conditions for new generations shaped on the values of the new.

The wound of modernity and the escape from history, as used by Serra, are in this sense two ways to define a moment of rupture in Western culture which, having rejected symbolic religious imagery replaced it by artistic creation with the weapon of a social and political commitment to act consciously throughout history.

The very refusal of the fathers was a rejection of lineal descent, with the consequent refusal of inheritance. Relativity and the fragmentary nature of facts, their easy reproducibility, became the characteristic that defined the modern. The modern which, as J. Clair defined it, *"Est moderne non-pas qui annonce ce qui vient, mais ce qui s'accorde, au sens musical du verbe, au moment. Moderne est ce qui trouve la mesure entre le temps qui vient de s'écouler et le temps qui va venir"*[32].

In the creation of the Futurist movement there was a deep contradiction between the dimension of consciousness and that of the will, as well as between history and artistic-imaginative tension.

I.1.c *Novelty and the Avant-Garde*

The sheer bombardment of words, images, actions, proclamations, and exhibitions of Futurism acted by breaking the sense of individuals' identity,

---

31   Ortega Y. Gasset, *Una interpretazione della storia universale*, in Maurizio Serra, *op. cit.*, p. 50.

32   Jean Clair, *La responsabilité de l'artiste* (Paris: Gallimard, 1997), p. 21.

thereby barring any form of continuity between past, present and future[33], and destroying the sense of life as a project.

It was in this sense that Frederic Jameson spoke of "multi-cerebral intensity": the result of the breaking of historical continuity understood as a union of emotion and reason, going to form mental subjects without balance between mind and body, from which arose the problem of the division of reality.

At this juncture, Futurism and all other avant-garde movements, as well as Surrealism, could shoulder a good deal of the responsibility, since they worked directly on the senses and not on the intellect which can insert critical filters.

The distinction between novelty and the avant-garde in the artistic field has a very precise connotation. Renaissance Art had surpassed previous art, the Impressionist canons had renewed Romantic painting creating a new organization of aesthetic codes, but were not described as *avant-garde*; avant-garde art arose as the art of destroying past canons, rejecting every call for continuity of styles, of sensibility for the eras that preceded it. The diversity of function and approach is therefore plain.

Novelty grants itself the possibility of laying its bases in a past and, starting from these, recreating a form that does not demolish the principles that preceded it, but surpasses them almost by historical and social necessity; instead, the avant-garde felt orphaned, did not recognize its fathers, rejected the present, and this rejection plunged into the origins of creation to recreate an 'original' and not an 'inherited' present. The creative act *par excellence*, which was not historical as a memory of the past, but was a historical act in the sense that it dropped into the present being lived.

Hence the error of interpreting the avant-garde as ahistorical, that it clashed with a way of history understood in the Nietzschean sense.

A certain excess of history [...] no longer allows a person to perceive and to act unhistorically. He then draws himself from the infinity of his horizon back into himself, into the smallest egotistical region...He probably achieves cleverness in this, but never wisdom. He permits himself inner conversations, calculates, and gets along well with the facts, does not boil over...the complete dedication of the personality to the world process.[34]

---

33   Cfr. Mike Featherstone, *La cultura dislocata* (Rome: SEAM, 1998).
34   Friederich Nietzsche, *Sull'utilità e il danno della storia per la vita* (Milan: Adelphi, 1974), p. 88. "We know what the study of history is capable of, when it is pre-eminent, we know only too well: to eradicate the strongest instincts of youth, i.e. ardour, obstinacy, forgetfulness of self and love."

Why did avant-garde art developed in the first years of the twentieth century? Art is the creative use of the senses, the organization of the imaginative capacity stimulated by contingency in a further impetus to surpass visible reality.

The artistic act of the avant-garde which combined social action with a creative action resulted in contradictory acts and produced an interruption in the generational flow of culture.

By observing the phenomenon from a sociological point of view, we know that, with an interruption, there occurred a progressive rupture of the mechanism of transgression-criticism-transcendence with which the power of the dominant interests of a society was reproduced. The sovereignty of those interests was assured using language, it too dominant, the recurrence of the same social figures recognized and 'categorized' effortlessly by the collective imagination.

In this sense, it stratified false knowledge and a false reality, through a repressive power necessary to maintain the dominant organization. By reiterating the order of the discourse constituted, of which Foucault spoke, we simply change the combinatorial mode of a criticism, but essentially, to be recognized as dominant, it too must observe the rules laid down by the order that makes it valid.

Artistic transgression is a sign, it is in a dialectical relationship with society but does not use the same order of language; wishing its re-entry to already be a repressive action.

Contemporary art, to be such, must "cancel the social contract", as Adorno affirms, it has to cease to be useful, and offer itself to transcendence as an act that tends to supersede the existing. Only this was art for Adorno and Horkheimer[35].

In Adorno and Horkheimer's discourse on art what we find is criticism of an act's 'use value'. The 'useful' act is defined as social, while one that is devoid of usefulness is eminently human. The creative act in this context does not appear; it can be included as an act that is outside usefulness, it assumes an educational functionality, which would make it an ideological act, but one that indicates a different path to the cognitive act, a chance for verification.

In this sense, the Futurist act, as an artistic act, was also partly ideological, since it integrated the role in itself, in the very self-perception of anticipation, and was also a creative act since it artistically re-created an

---

35   Franco Riccio (ed.), T.W. Adorno; M. Horkheimer, *I seminari della Scuola di Francoforte. Protocolli di discussione*, (Milan: Franco Angeli, 1999), p. 156.

order of language, and was therefore functional to its role but not directly to society. Or better, it was a negative act given that it deconstructed to reconstruct. We can therefore say that Futurist avant-garde act was: Social, since it was part of a context where it acted and operated as an active minority; Creative, since it made up new rules for a new order of language; Ideological, since it presented itself as a cultural re-educator; and an act of cognitive opening, thus avant-garde in the direction of opening towards a mode and concept of a broader, non-academic, non-elitist culture.

Marinetti's work did not appear from nothing: the use of manifestos for cultural propaganda had been widely used in France for some years; in Italy, *macchinolatria* or machine worship had already been declaimed on several occasions and under several guises by Mario Morasso, with *Il Nuovo Aspetto Meccanico del Mondo* published in 1907, or even *Uomini e Idee del Domani*. *L'egoarchia* was published in 1898, and was thus substantially attributable to a period contemporary or immediately prior to Marinetti's production.

Marinetti had been able to gather many ideas on contemporary art during his stays in Paris, which was the centre of the cultural ferment of the time; thus, we cannot say that Marinetti was actually the inventor of a new art, on the other hand, in sociology, the term 'invention' is perhaps non-existent, in the sense that in social dynamics nothing emerges from the wilderness, social forces are alternated, transformed and recur, without which society itself could not exist.

Of Marinetti, what we can say is that he was a revolutionary in the strictly sociological sense, a cultural revolutionary who entered the social crisis caused by the change in the industrial age and imposed new processes on it.

Marinetti's revolt was not the kind that is defined in sociology as "a riot of the visceral type": potential material for a revolution, but still at a disorganized embryonic stage, that can lead to simple, albeit violent protest. It was a revolution in culture: it had a programme, a doctrine, and an army of artists in its wake. It had everything to enter the cultural context and impose/propose an approach to culture that organized every aspect.

In this sense, the Futurist avant-garde was the most complete and better organized movement than any other contemporary European one. Paradoxically, its organization, its ways of communication and its production status, made it being not a 'novelty' nor 'revolt', but a revolutionary vanguard.

With a project, a doctrine, and an army.

As already mentioned, the social roots of Marinetti's cultural education were sunk in the Milanese upper middle classes. He was born in Alexandria in Egypt, at the time an Italian colony for trade with Africa, (the circle of Italian intellectuals known as *Casa Rossa* was from Alexandria), he studied at Jesuit Colleges, although he got himself expelled thanks to readings deemed inconsistent with the curriculum, such as Zola's naturalist novels; he was always intrigued by the news, social change, art and literature, but rejected a substantial distance from practical action.

In this sense, Marinetti believed he could change mankind, starting from culture, language, literature, and art. Consequently, Marinetti's utopia clashed with various criticisms and observations; from this utopia, it was but a short step to an ideological vision of culture.

According to Adorno: "The request to impose the values of culture on men is always ideological, the primary needs of men do not lie in this direction," despite any criticism of the cultural system, in the statement that "the artificiality of man increases through the fact that he becomes the product of his own products"[36], and Avant-gardes were caught up in this game trying to make become society the product of their ideas.

If the ideological risk of a revolution through the cultural indoctrination of the individual might be acceptable, what was not acceptable was the observation that would be made later by the culture industry, thanks to which culture was emptied of its cognitive power and thus, later, of a way to act.

Through the symbolic nature and transcendence of the act, art can be elected as transgressive in a dialectic with the culture it rejects and from which it is generated, for example.

Theoretical and social analyses cannot enter a context by denying it, since in so doing they would deny their own validity and existence.

Instead, art can do so, indeed this is how it becomes a symbolic gesture and passes beyond the material meaning. It can, through a symbolic gesture in contention with the social structure, turn itself into a transgressive and revolutionary act.

Consequently, within the discussions of the Frankfurt School, there were many debates on need, value, art and culture, which, unable to exceed the limit of the useful and the acknowledged, without the remained speculations sometimes.

Confronting the production of avantagardes there is such a rejection of rationality within that negative artistic gesture which, by assuming its transcendence from a context, became symbolic communication, and finally achieved universality through expression.

Paradoxically, the scientific-rational-critical appraoch of the Frankfurt School, in its yearning to explain a denial, could hardly follow the use of language of the avant-garde revolution. It seems now, with the time, that it

---

36   Adorno and Horkheimer, ibid., p. 157.

could not help remaining much more abstract than the gesture of negation by the avant-garde.

Marinetti's avant-garde can be summed up as the ability to connect the social situations he observed through artistic activity; a utopia that could change the world not with new structures as alternatives to the preceding ones, but by destroying them and returning to the individual freedom of experimentation, a flexibility of expression at times without any practical use.

Exactly what the Frankfurt School identified as the only condition that could urge culture to transcend the existing: thereby abandoning the utilitarian contract of capitalist society, is exactly what criticism alone does not and cannot do, but expression in the guise of artistic act can succeed.

"Art that withdraws from the results of practices can assume an aspect that is transcendent in the direction of a classless society"[37].

Criticism cannot abandon language, cannot explain except through the established order, while avant-garde art contests the language in its form of domination, as in Foucaultian's reflection. Arts can be only a sign, a sudden refuse, a non rationally explained gesture.

Individual and social growth through the possibility of error, the machine was the tool of the future that predicted the new speed of society, the aeroplane was predicting liberation of expression from conventional and stylistic bonds, the train was becoming the unconditional extension of communication through which the future world would overcome social barriers.

Individually, no new technical instrument was exalted merely because it was new, but because it already saw in which direction it would influence existence. In all of this, Marinetti's ability lay in capturing the lightness of this new type of life rather than the negative quality it necessarily bore.

In 1907, Boccioni wrote in his diary:

> It seems to me that art and artists are today in conflict with science. [...] Now the great heart and great minds of humanity are heading towards a visibility that is made of precision and accuracy and positivism. The vast analysis that our century has made has renewed us, creating specialists; this explains the lack of universality in the modern era[38],

so, on the one hand futurists were well aware of complexity and their was an attempt to recapture universalism and complexity in a society were specialization was dominating social awareness. This is why, avant-garde

---

37   Adorno and Horkheimer, ibid., p. 156.
38   Umberto Boccioni, *Pittura e scultura futuriste* (Milan, SE, 1997), p. 77.

recognized a kind of "superiority" of science in relation to art as owner of that rigour which made it closer to contemporary sensibilities. In this way, the art of yesteryear that sought emotion in sentimentalism found itself speaking a dead language that was no longer comprehensible.

But while science has strict rules that steer it, linked mainly to the results, art is formed in relation to what attracts, and finds its creative instinct in this dialectic.

In the dialectic between man and machine, the Futurists saw a liberating solution for the evolution of sensibility. In relation to the machine, art could learn the new language of modernity and, through this language, communicate the changed difficulties of adaptation of the individual through new tools.

Science innovated and specialized the intellect with technology, art entered a direct relationship with technology and carried out the reverse process of adapting the spirit to the new reality.

Marinetti prophetically intuited that the new culture would be largely technological, and it was on the wave of this lucid awareness that he assumed an ambivalent role between art and politics; from the very first Futurist Manifesto of 1909 it took only a few years of political change for Marinetti to vanish into fictitious isolation. Futurist art continued, but had been voided, its initial effectiveness and vigour downsized by compromise.

A Futurist work was created in relation to the spectator, if it managed to disturb, upset, overturn sensations and shuffle order, then it had the right to be a part of Futurist works.

This was a kind of art that was institutionalized through the spectator, and even more so through his or her reaction. "Our social effort is to build a new moral," Settimelli maintained. However, Settimelli's reproach of Croce's criticism would appear in some parts to have been played with the same cards: "Being defined barbarians by a redskin is a qualification of authentic civilization! But how come this piece of philosophical lard wants to deal with poetry? By now everyone always wants to talk about what they don't know! Proud of what they don't possess!"[39]

From this point of view, aware artists could be skilful manipulators of souls rather than of minds, the need they felt to swap opinions with and measure themselves against other sensibilities made them skilful in contacting the outside, without which they risked death. The words of Max Ernst could not be clearer:

---

39   Emilio Settimelli, *Marinetti. L'uomo e l'artista* (Milan: Edizioni Futuriste di "Poesia", 1921), p. 79.

In New York, to meet, you had to call and make an appointment in advance. And the pleasure of meeting was sapped before it took place. Consequently, in N.Y. we had artists but no art. Art is not the product of a single artist but many. At a high level, it is the product of an exchange of ideas. It's impossible for an artist to work in a vacuum.[40]

Futurism was the avant-garde movement that opened the door for all other avant-garde movements.

In the archives, Papini located a letter by Marinetti from March 1913 in which the latter complained about the presumed plagiarism by Apollinaire of some of Futurism's ideas, passing them off as his own.

"The *Orphiques* ideas, presented in the *Bernheim* catalogue," Marinetti said, "and contested by Apollinaire himself and by the Cubists on the importance of the subject in the painting, were the principles of the movement that Apollinaire borrowed from Futurism without mentioning the origin." Thus, Marinetti asked for room to be left in the review *Lacerba* for Boccioni's answer.

Thanks to this publication, Marinetti would come into direct contact with Apollinaire, with whom he had already spent some of his Parisian evenings.

On 29 June 1913, a document appeared signed by Guillaume Apollinaire entitled *L'Antitradition Futuriste*, which, after being sent promptly to Marinetti, became a Manifesto and went into print, thus becoming the French manifesto that recognized to all effects the Italian avant-garde as the force promoting the artistic renewal in Europe[41]. All of this happened four years after the official birth of the movement, datable from the publication of the first Manifesto.

Marinetti's dispute with the French artists was fed precisely in reaction to the initial ambiguity of the position of Apollinaire, who, on the one hand "animated by me and Boccioni showed Picasso the innovative energy of Futurist works exalting movement and modernolatry"[42], on the other, almost seemed to be mocking it by aping its exalted tones.

Among the European avant-garde movements, it was Dadaism that became spiritually consumed first. Apart from anything else, the Dadaist trend was arguably the most radical of all the avant-garde movements. The

---

40   Marcel Jean, *Autobiografia del Surrealismo* (Rome: Ed. Riuniti, 1983).
41   Guillaume Apollinaire, *Lettere a F.T. Marinetti*, Paolo A. Jannini (ed.) (Fiesole: C.D.A.S. "Le Coste", 1978).
42   *Ibid.*, p. 9.

absolute negation of every form of life, art, politics and society increased its subversive potential, but also prevented propaganda on any front.

Dadaism was deliberately a form of expression without a future. In this sense, for Dada we can speak of a movement of revolt, but one that exhausted itself in protest. In Dada lay negation, which was already a criticism of society, but it lacked a project or doctrine.

Like the other avant-garde movements, the Dadaist group had no interventionist character, and was often criticized as decadent aestheticism: in November 1916, while the Battle of Verdun was ending, the Galerie Dada opened at Eingang Tiefenhöfe in Zurich. The land of Verdun was barely large enough to hold the fallen.

While Hugo Ball and his companion Emy Hennings were producing *Krippen Spiele* (nursery games) with acting dolls, the decimation of the Italian Army began. On 18 May 1916, Ball noted in his diary that Tristan Tzara was thinking intensely of how to create a review to propagate Dadaist ideas ("Tzara is tormented by the review"); in those same hours, a second lieutenant, a sergeant and eight troops belonging to the 141st Italian infantry, chosen for decimation, were accused of defeatism and cowardice and were executed by order of the regiment's commander.

"Defeatism and cowardice": this branding might also apply to those intellectuals and artists who gathered in Zurich from various parts of Europe to take part in the Dadaist protest. A poetic and moral protest, against the war certainly, but substantially "neutral". *Déraciné* in every sense, the Dadaist "takes no stance for any ideology or any regime"[43].

Apart from anything else, the Futurist position was anything but neutral:

> But condoning defeatism and cowardice was not insignificant in a Europe that was all 'heroic' and nationalistic. Secondly, and this is the essential thing, the ideological-political scope of an artistic movement has never been the same thing (sometimes it has even been the contrary) as the explicit ideological positions of its members. [...] Dada drastically introduced into the century's cultural issues an element that would never leave, and that it would be appropriate to remember every time certain questions pop up again. This element is *negation*, or if we wish, the negative pole of the dialectic, which has usefully continued to operate until today.[44]

---

43   Lucio Villari, *Dada contro tutti nell'Europa in guerra*, in "La Repubblica", 15 December 1976.

44   Enrico Filippini, reply to Lucio Villari, *Dada: la sua negazione non è mai finita...*, "La Repubblica", 21 December 1976.

Surrealism was born officially in the autumn of 1924, and in its artistic evolution ended up politically supporting the credo of the Third Communist International.

I shall not deal with the intimate relationship between Surrealism and politics, but immediate reflection certainly indicates that for Surrealism the adhesion to Communism was a search for external protection, while in the relationship between Futurism and Fascism, the relationship remained extremely confused.

It is true that many convictions coincided with certain aspects of the Fascist credo: the myths of strength, action and Italianness, for example. However, the internal structure of the movement guaranteed it a substantial artistic autonomy scarcely adaptable to gregarious forms.

While the political aspect of an era is necessarily historical, an artistic movement such as Futurism, despite its deep historical matrix, saved and rediscovered its spiritual side in some less vehement words, but perhaps precisely because of this, with a greater potential to enter the history books.

Ironically, it was precisely the main credo of Futurism: art should be an expression limited to a precise historical, social, and economic lapse of time, and as such prone to being replaced in just few years by younger expressiveness, which created the movement's strength and perpetuity.

Its spirituality consisted in this precise aspect, the ability to have ended an indispensable truth of the modern age: the transiency of expression, despite its importance in defining the sensibility of an arc of time. This leads us to think that the speed of turnover of a contemporary artistic phenomenon is not only assessed based on its artists' inability to close an epoch even ten years later, but rather in the epoch's inability to give rise to that same expressiveness only ten years later.

For Marinetti, what slowed down the evolution of an era was reasoning; intelligence had slower times than intuition since it tried to fix what was in motion, so much so that by the time it had managed to do so, the sensibility was elsewhere and far from being rationally explicable.

Art will pass over the idea. It is the idea that carries the past. It fixes perceptions, gives a logical form that allows them to last for the brains. Marinetti hates intelligence. The idea may prove useful: encoding invention. But, wishing to be eternal by definition, it puts off following its evolution; marching at a slower pace, it empties itself of content. Is intuition going to replace it? In fact, Marinetti was not Bergsonian. Intuition is a most effective form of intelligence. Futurism appeals, firstly, to feeling.[45]

It is for the poet to open the doors of the senses to an immediate, direct, virgin perception of the world. He will penetrate the essence of matter, he will throw himself into the chaos of noise, weights and odours and cause them to gush forth.

Marinetti's Futurism was performing an hyperbolic capacity to create images at the limit of paradox, the only possible language for a revolution with overstating expressions without which it would not have had its irrepressible destabilising impact.

Each prophetic vision or intuition, although rooted in reality, was always a reality to come, therefore, to overcome the givenness of its condition, it could only leap towards the future, unleashing the necessary reaction of refusal that we always find in the face of a violent event.

In any case, in these words is the description of an era with deeply spiritual needs, but detached from the religious vision, aiming at a religion of life rooted in a daily attitude, being considered spirituality as the faculty of human progress.

---

45   Emilio Settimelli, *Marinetti. L'uomo e l'artista* (Milan: ed. Futurist "Poetry", 1921), pp. 90-92, (Continued) "In short, and this explains why it could be more absolute in painting and music, the less abstract arts, Futurism would be more rightly called *Presenteismo*. It is the arrogance of the surroundings, or [...] a lyrical psychology of matter. [...]
The advent of the complete renovation of the principles of expression, shape, evasion from the straitjackets of reasoning language.
A deeply Latin spirit, therefore a builder, Marinetti, such an enemy of logic, built a system of flawless logic above it. It is elsewhere on this point that Apollinaire, the cubists, others more clever than deep, mainly borrowed from him.
Inspiration obeys the law of speed. Expression should therefore abandon everything that slows it down and makes it heavy. Abolition of conjunctions that discursively spellbind. The substance is not discursive. The suppression of adjectives, those dogs of the noun and the adverbs, their clothes hangers. They inhibit the flight of the imagination. Use of nouns, randomly, as they were born, with the double that they evoke by analogy (man-torpedo boat, woman-roadstead, piazza-funnel). Use of verbs in the infinitive to avoid subjecting the noun to the writer's *I*.
Abolition of punctuation. Extension of analogies. Introduction of mathematical signs, $+, \times, -, =$, etc. and of different typefaces, to give the impression of movement of life. All these modifications in traditional syntax were summarized in the title of the 14th Futurist Manifesto: Wireless Imagination and Words-in-Freedom [...] Their authors had forgotten only two things: to cite Marinetti and to feed off the fertilizing romanticism that constituted the essential part of its innovation."

The artistic skills of every man would be developed, solving the problem of wellbeing with spirituality: "We shall have the artistic solution for the social problem"[46].

Thereby revealing to man his inner capacity for change, spiritually-oriented satisfaction. The spiritual impulse must be fed and nourished for an individual to be well balanced, but everything must be differentiated from religion in the sense of an obligation, to become an inner necessity.

The Futurist revolt was against concepts. Subverting the representation of the world as determined by the dominant culture, this was the guiding thread that connected all the violent Futurist events, and this was the intention: demolish the certainties, demolish the usual process of constructing reality through the cancellation of references that served to ensure this process which the common man, if he never questioned the correctness of the values referred to, limited himself to enacting.

Above all, Marinetti criticized the habits of everyday life: the way of eating, the propensity to emotion, the concept of women, restricted by a mainly masculine dominant vision, with the consequence of causing a flawed relationship between man and woman.

Marinetti's work concerned a substantial "skimming" from Italian sentimentalism, which he considered a chaotic mixture of religious devotion, intellectual dependence, ignorance and a substantial lack of social organization that blocked any emancipation of the individual.

For Marinetti, sentimentality was the intellectual ballast of Italians. He urged the Venetians to free themselves and to liberate their city from the sentimentality that denied it any progress. For the Futurists, Venice was the capital and symbol of Romantic decadence.

Deeply nationalistic, the Futurist movement burrowed carefully into the most typical flaws of the country's nature and social organization, combating any resistance. This does not detract from the fact that the result was exactly the most easily predictable one; in the collective memory, Futurism remained a blatant artistic movement that was very little understood. In it, the passion typical of the Latin world, to be constructive and not get lost in lust and inconclusiveness, had to be channelled into more current ideals: beauty and woman must no longer be the inseparable combination, if others could be created.

This passion could be directed to several things: the multiplicity of passions, the fragmentation of affectivity allowed its distribution on various

---

46   Enrico Settimelli, *Marinetti. L'uomo e l'artista* (Milan: ed. Futurist "Poetry", 1921), pp. 90-92.

fronts, women should no longer be essential in the life of men, they must be merely one of the beautiful things we can enjoy.

Mankind multiplied, the senses multiplied, were infected by several stimuli and enriched the perception of the environment in several gradations, relationships became mechanical and the kingdom of the machine emerged triumphant. Another type of beauty took place in the collective imagination, in this case, masculine: the beauty of the machine. Beauty was transforming into the sublime through power of the machine.

Here, Futurism showed its historical limit. Despite intuition inducing it to operate culturally on planes devoid of sexual distinction and to approach considerations of individual freedom, thus transforming the distinction between the sexes into a distinction between people, it showed its profound linguistic dependence in the uncertainty of the genus of the automobile, and in the need to shift sexual desire from "women" to the car. Admission of its limits thus occurred through a demonstration of the linguistic prison, which, despite everything, shrouded its depths.

In certain manifestations, Futurism seemed to approach an awareness of history that exalted its artists, but they were also willingly and lucidly defeated from the outset: they spilled their blood in the name of a progress which they knew well they would never see at the forefront.

I.1.d *Theories of the Avant-Garde*

There has been many possible explanation of the concept of avant-garde art, less in sociology than in philosophical speculations. Considering a prediction starting from its fulfilment seems the most fitting and self-validating process.

Have the theories on art declaimed by Futurism come true?

The problem of today's art is that of not having found a position that fits its reality. Within the context of institutional conceptualisations, it seems to be closed in a duality that restrains the universality that would appear due; the conceptions that dominate it can be reduced to two: art as a work of art; art as communication.

And this duality only imposes the question as a reduction to art as a work or art as a reality. This is the dreaded *flattening* of artistic creation by social analysts or even by the critics, a concept that considers the autonomy of the work while leaving its value to be considered independently from the environment that feeds and generates it; and a second conception which reduces art to a gimmick, losing both its specificity and its contents, besides its solemnity.

Contemporary art is often associated with transgressive art. And this is certainly a commonplace that we owe to the superficial reception given to the work of the avant-garde. Contemporary art is thus associated with a model of transgression, violence, and extremism, but we cannot confine a work, even if of strong tones, to the mere way it was expressed. And this is true in both one sense and the other: can't be said avant-garde art as being merely unconventional and, at the same time, not every transgressive artwork is a work of avant-garde art. Certainly, the difficulty lies in finding the modes of art and those of avant-garde art beyond transgression.

Reasoning on the assumption that art wishes to transgress already implies a classification, a category from which the observation of art is deprived of the possibility to understand, since it perverts the essence of the object of study *a priori*.

New art shifted its interest onto new subjects: the relationship and the process. The nub of the entire Futurist production consisted in this shifting of the subject from a social context with fixed references to a social mode made up of negotiation, interpretation, and transformation of reality. According to Adorno "In sharp contrast to traditional art, new art accents the once hidden element of being something made, something produced. (…) From this arose the pleasure of substituting for the artworks the process of their own production"[47], and this changed also the relevancy of a work of art, what Benjamin already faced in the German baroque drama, because for most of these movements the core issue was not to create great artworks, but to produce an attitude to it, in which "the essence of the provocation may be sought in in the preponderance of art over the artwork"[48]

Marinetti entered a relationship with his future audience through Manifestos in which he pronounced the intentions of this new art with the necessary impetus. Why did he speak instead of beginning to administer his intentions only through artworks? Why wait for the visual perception of the public to come into line with the new? Did their habits sheepishly fit his art as they did earlier art? Perhaps more than disseminating art, the idea was to disseminate a message. And to be received, this message had to fall on awareness.

Fortunato Depero was clear about Futurism's mode of proceeding; he said that the public was to be "catechized" to new art, and therefore

---

47   Theodor W. Adorno, *Aesthetic Theory* (Minneapolis: University of Minnesota Press, 1997), p. 26.
48   Theodor W. Adorno, *Aesthetic Theory* (Minneapolis: University of Minnesota Press, 1997), p. 25.

a content message, Manifestos, had to complement an artwork in order to explain the idea and the process to produce it. Consent and taste were created. A verbal explanation that would be a parallel text to the exhibition of the works was needed so that the distance between the perception of art and everyday life should be shortened. People had become accustomed to a perceptual work in reverse and found themselves having to associate real life with the artistic one. The present had already been transformed into the future. Reception could resolve into a flash of awareness.

In this sense, the talk was of a contemporary art that raised the problematic nature of the role and functionality of art in social organization. But its intention did not end here.

In *The Theory of the Avant-Garde*, R. Poggioli observed this phenomenon in a systematic way: the avant-garde concept, the difference between the school and the movement, the activism and antagonism of the avant-garde. But perhaps the contribution that will be most useful to this study is the definition of the avant-garde as the birth of a concept of art aware of its historicity:

> In the case of contemporary art, the hypothesis that it existed before the age that coined its name is a twofold anachronistic error, since it considers the past as a function of the present and the future. An authentic avant-garde cannot arise unless the current concept emerges, at least in its potency: and it is evident that this concept or its equivalents were presented to the historical western consciousness only in our age, whose more remote temporal limits are preludes of the romantic experience.[49]

In these terms, this kind of art becomes an awareness of art both in a historical period, and on the potential of the artistic tool. The artistic tool in the avant-garde became a gesture, according to Poggioli, and "in many cases the avant-garde can be said to be more interested in movement than creation"[50], the gesture in this case being distinguished from the action, which implies an intentionality in its implementation. Thus, for Poggioli, there was seemingly no idea of an avant-garde as the protagonist of an action, but as a performer of a historical necessity, which in the given period was interpreted more easily by an artistic movement.

If, however, on reading further, we find that "while the school is inconceivable outside the humanistic ideal, of the idea of culture as a

---

49   Renato Poggioli, *Teoria dell'arte d'avanguardia* (Bologna: il Mulino, 1962), p. 26.
50   *Ibid.*, p. 40.

Thesaurus: instead, a movement conceives culture not as an increase but as creation, or at least deals with it as a centre of activity or of energy"[51].

We find, then, the explanation for a theory of contemporary art as a different mode of action, which gives importance to the multiplicity of the "gestures", as Poggioli called them, to give life to wider action, inserted in a movement for creation and not out of erudition. The apparently insignificant gesture takes its meaning in the light of its creative concatenation, many gestures are the result of an artistic action freed from manner and, because of this, more sensitive to changes in the present it embodies. Being the "gesture" the corrrispondent to the contemporary idea of "performance". The modern in art acts, then, as the contemplation of itself in the context, its self-criticism, as P. Bürger defined it in *Theory of the Avant-Garde*.

This position would then be proposed as a premise for a kind of art that expresses with its own means, the work and the propaganda, a radical criticism in its relationship with society and more profoundly, with art as an institution. The criticism was thus more targeted, shifted the responsibility from the artist with regard to the work, to a responsibility of awareness, of the relationship that binds to institutions.

I.2 *The Modern and Postmodern in Art*

In *The Predicament of Culture*[52], J. Clifford writes, in a chapter on ethnographic surrealism in the notes presenting the study, about a possible research on a common ground between the avant-garde and social sciences as an area that is still underdeveloped. Despite this, he said he considered it a "little-explored trail of a crucial modern orientation towards cultural order"[53]. This cultural order was "not distinctly defined. It can be more adequately defined modernist rather than modern, identifying the core of the problem – and opportunity – in the fragmentation and juxtaposition of cultural values"[54]. Avant-garde art ended up embodying the status of culture and aesthetics: valorization of the fragment, paradoxical and surprising contradictions, exaltation of particular situations such as those dominated by eroticism, the exotic and the unconscious. Surrealism was the liberation

---

51   *Ibid.*, p. 43.
52   James Clifford, *The Predicament of Culture* (Harvard: Harvard University Press, 1988), p. 101.
53   *Ibid.*, p. 101.
54   *Ibid.*, p. 102.

of the unconscious through artistic means; the theoretical construction of Freudian psychoanalysis had made its mark on the artistic imagination allowing the unconscious reactions to stimuli of a social organization that had suddenly changed to emerge without organization or order.

But social time has changed.

The industrial economy accelerated domestic production and by lowered costs, opened up national borders to trade with foreign countries. The same borders which are now trying to close again all over the world. The consequences of the mechanization of work in the textile industry and the development of the steel industry based on the use of coal, increased production by 100 or 200 times, and the actual price of yarns decreased considerably.

From a political point of view, the changing of America, at the time a main European colony, to a set of economically autonomous independent states redefined the resources and attitude of European production and policy both inside the various countries and at an inter-European level[55].

Industrialization launched economic liberalism as a first impact, protectionism in periods of greater economic crisis, but a constant opening up towards foreign countries, either through Expos, or with the travels of exportation.

In this context, much of the cultural openness was also down to colonial exhibitions and trade with importing countries.

The great Expos that appeared increasingly frequently in those years were vast containers for updates on foreign production with the possibility of exchanging products with greater public acceptance.

These same exhibitions hosted cultural projects from the countries of origin of the products being exchanged, and were a source of cultural curiosities not only for traders, who benefited from the point of view of an alignment of their production with neighbouring countries, but were also a place of cultural curiosities for artists and intellectuals who could observe and contact "exotic" cultures and manifestations without travelling.

Antonin Artaud saw Balinese dancing for the first time at the 1931 colonial fare in Paris, from which he understood better his own idea of theatre as a bridge between East and West, which until then had remained deprived of any validation and was therefore solely theoretical.

---

55   Cf. Paul Bairoch, *Le politiche commerciali in Europa dal 1815 al 1914*, in *"Storia Economica Cambridge"*, *Le economie industriali*, vol. VIII, (Turin: Einaudi, 1992).

Consequently, modernity presented itself as the bearer of a different relationship between space, time and institutions, and all of this involved a rethinking of social categories. A rethinking that can be seen as reflectivity:

> What characterizes modernity is marked by the hunger for novelty, but perhaps this is not entirely accurate. What characterizes modernity is not the fact of embracing novelty in itself, but the assumption of a global reflectivity, which obviously includes reflection on the nature of the reflection itself. [...] But this idea is convincing only until we note that the reflectivity of modernity in reality subverts reason, at least where we intend reason as acquisition of a certain knowledge.[56]

From the point of view of social action, modernity was defined by Simmel as the epoch in which a crisis takes on a character of normality[57]. In this way, modernity revealed itself as a crucial moment in which the tension of the relationship between the individual and society, the conflict between the need for the self-fulfilment of the individual and his or her social being, could not find a solution[58].

The differentiation required for metropolitan life launched a profound process of distancing between the needs of the individual and the structural ones of maintaining formal social organization. In short, it implemented a corrosion phenomenon within that emerged through the backwash of the so-called "irrational", but which was actually nothing more than the most elementary and primitive search for a sense of belonging and identity of the individual, who, as a single person, could not be found in the broad and depersonalized context of the metropolises, places that promoted a dialectic between private life and social life. The confirmation of Tönnies theorization about the difference between *Gemeinschaft* and *Gesellschaft*.

This interpretation finds support in the intuitions of Simmel, who showed that "concretely, the ambivalent dynamic of the relationship man/society, in the tension between the complexity assumed by the systems of determination, which if, for some aspects, seem to favour the expansion of individual self-realization, for others, tends to disintegrate it"[59].

Hence, the modern condition was more and more characterized by major historical breakdowns, by fragments, by ambiguity and procedures that introduced, both in art and in literature, the image of "creative

---

56 Anthony Giddens, *The Consequences of Modernity*, (Standford: Standford University Press, 1991), p. 40.
57 Georg Simmel, *Il conflitto della civiltà moderna*, (Turin: F.lli Bocca Ed., 1925), p. 37.
58 *Ibid.*
59 Franco Crespi, *Teoria dell'agire sociale* (Bologna: il Mulino, 1999), p. 234.

destruction"[60], given that artistic creation had a capacity given by its own quality of *immateriality*: it was beyond good and evil[61].

> Being modern means finding ourselves in an environment that promises us adventure, power, joy, growth, transformation of ourselves and of the world; and which at the same time, threatens to destroy everything we have. Environments and modern experiences transcend all ethnic and geographic divisions, of class and nationality, religion and ideology: in this sense, we can truly say that they unite all mankind, a unity in separateness.[62]

With its anti-traditional character, art unmasked the futility of daily life, accepted the challenge of modernity, assumed the fleeting and ephemeral as *place*. The historical avant-garde movements were the artistic equivalent of modernity, it would seem from Clifford's convictions, on the fragmented nature of the modern, but this does not explain the absolute abandonment of the modern to the fragment, the "dissolving", against the "full-steam-ahead" theorization of the avant-garde[63].

Theorization is a feature of all the historical avant-garde movements, since their operation was ultimately based on a contempt for the present. The desire not to exist *in* and *for* the present, but only in a projection *towards* a future they would never know but of which they could be called the creators, was both the weakness and the strength of the avant-garde.

The rejection of the present as a thought structure, but not as a practical existence, allows a glimpse of the movement's double face. On one hand, the exuberant and the lofty, devoid of roots and links with the past, from which ideas were reprocessed, but, we would also be forced to acknowledge, an inheritance. On the other, the underground work on unconscious images, on the interiorization of roles and expectations towards art but also towards society, language, politics and communication.

A winning strategy, it would seem, since one century later we are still wondering about these issues, but above all we realize that they have become reality beneath our eyes.

What was the impetus of Futurism – merely utopia? In this sense, G. Lista totally discards the image of an unrealistic and irrational voluntarism in the negative sense of the word; it is not about a utopia for Futurism,

---

60   Cfr. David Harvey, *op. cit.*, p. 30.
61   *Ibid.*, p. 33.
62   Marshall Berman in David Harvey, *The Condition of Postmodernity*, (Hoboken: Wiley-Blackwell, 1990), p. 19.
63   Antoine Compagnon, *op. cit.*, p. 72.

but a profound faith in action as defining of the individual and his or her identity. A faith rooted in the sacred texts of oriental religions, through which Marinetti saw in action the principle of evolution in cosmic life.

For Marinetti, action was the only tool the individual had to ensure a future, with all its apparent ambiguities. Over time, an action continues to be talked about, and in this, he was not mistaken. But equally, we can see clearly that the action of which Marinetti spoke was "theatrical", cathartic, not experiential and woven out of relationships with others. Perhaps it was here that the Futurist structure began to waver.

The theatrical action affects the unconscious, affects the organization of reality, but it is always a "laboratory" action protected from the context, not immersed in life, and therefore, as such, when it enters in correlation with it, it lapses.

This is the threshold for the division between art and life, this is the limit and the wealth of art, but if we do not bear this in mind we enter art as a game of life, in the conscious irresponsibility of not fully entering the social context, but wishing to change it through imagination.

For Gottfried Benn, every era had its initial phase of growth and its moment of decline, this decline stage being marked by artistic fertility[64]. Indeed, art represents the final moment of evolution, which is a prelude to the crisis to lay the foundations of a new civilization. Art is therefore the processing time, the period that is useless and fundamental at the same time. Materially and visually useless, since it does not make progress that is exterior but interior, in the face and vision of which everything must be rebuilt and rethought.

In this sense, the postmodern moment can be considered the creative appendix of the modern era, the space in which everything was possible, the same structure of thought was staked in pragmatically emptying the dialectic of meaning; the moment when the interpersonal relationship as a fruit of the dialectic had exploded due to a dissolution of the meaning of words as signifiers and not as signifieds.

Seen from the outside, the postmodern seems an opposite of the modern which however is unable to be truly such: opposition would be foolish; its

---

64   Gottfried Benn, *Lo smalto sul nulla*, (Milan: Adelphi, 1992). "There is always an order through which we look into the abyss, an order that grasps life in a tidily divided space, chasing it with hammer blows, grips it with a chisel, engraves it with a flame on a vessel in the figure of yoked bulls – an order in which the material of the earth and the spirit of man, again intertwined and coupled, or even in fierce mutual challenge, will elaborate what our glances, today so stunned, are looking for: art; that which is perfect".

antagonism would remain subordinate [...] the whole of Andy Warhol's work is based on this tension between modern and postmodern [...] The unique artistic action possible consists in producing something that takes up the forms in an exaggerated way only to sweep them away, placing them in another context that is both similar and different with respect to the point of departure.[65]

The mode typical of the postmodern artistic action seems to be to absorb the images of advanced capitalism and anti-capitalism, using the very materials and forms of society to ridicule them[66].

In another way, Bürger sought to define the position of art in the contemporary age by saying that a work will no longer be linked to modern society thanks to the world it represents, but only because it denies, in the concept of form, a rationality that obeys the rules and criteria[67].

In essence, we have returned to the concept of modern art as an art of destruction, however, Bürger opposed the plurality of artistic materials coexisting without the primacy of one with respect to the other and offered to the free availability of the artist.

Materials no longer had a status of privilege, as the avant-garde movements of the beginning of the century believed, for example in music, but a juxtaposition of materials that had reached a certain level of maturity, in differentiated ways within each artistic practice. None of which matched Warhol's conception of art and its function.

The ultimate explanation of the artist and critic described by Perniola does not concur with Bürger's analysis, which instead seems to sit on a different level: what is required is a rereading of some major texts that founded modernity outside the categories of traditional literary history without subjecting it to commonly admitted classifications, for example, in playing on the opposition between realism and naturalism; on the other hand, this very rereading works as a denouncement of postmodern commonplaces that tended to reduce the works of the past to a state of cultural knowledge in an undifferentiated way; it was there that the urgency lay[68].

Much of the production of French Deconstructionism, from Deleuze and Guattari to the philosophy of Derrida and the studies of Lacan, performed a careful analysis of the thought structures of the postmodern current, without leaving, in addition to many complex and often indecipherable comments, also net clarifications of contemporary social phenomena, grasping the structure of

---

65   Mario Perniola, *L'arte e la sua ombra* (Turin: Einaudi, 2000), p. 42.
66   *Ibid.*, p. 42.
67   Peter Bürger, *La prose de la modernité* (Paris : Klincksieck, 1994), p. 10.
68   Cf. Peter Bürger, *op. cit.*, p. 11.

behaviour as prophetic of future society, such as the nomadic, or the central thesis of *Anti-Oedipus*, according to which desire is always revolutionary, a machine ever ready to destroy the reassuring solidity provided by power.

In relation to the machine, the individual in the new era also became a machine but a desirous one, and only through this quality of the intellect connected with the prospect of pleasure, did he or she manage to erode the modern productive system that demands order and continuity equal to that of the machine.

Here too, a part of Foucault's work is called into question, especially concerning the power of language and its constitutionally acceptable order or disorder. Hence the postmodern game of the articulation posthumous to the destruction of values in different creative operations of construction and planning, that were not so much utopian as aesthetic, the emerging value at the basis of future society being aesthetics.

While the problem of the preceding age related to the machine as a new element, as an "extension of the human arm" in McLuhan's words, the postmodern era developed a creative phase of the pure idleness of the tool, language itself lost every dryness in syntax and meaning to enter the virtuosity of thought, in the architecture of an aesthetic design that proposed its identity in this value.

At this point, we cannot avoid an in-depth analysis of the change in importance and significance of the aesthetic term.

Once again, for an observer of social phenomena, the problem of the study of the aesthetic term can only provide a practical approach, arguably too simplistic, undoubtedly with philosophical ideas and cues, but tending to an approach of the phenomenon based essentially on its observable consequences in the social order or change.

From a micro-social point of view, both Futurism and Marinetti were above all a revolt against the old Italy, against traditional values, they too so aged that they had become pseudo values. From a macro point of view, they assumed the coordinates of a necessity for cosmic expression and communication as well as a contesting new power at hand for individuals.

Karel Teige observed: "Before Futurism, Italy was oppressed by a heavy stagnation that had lasted for more than half a century: at the time, Italy was nothing but one of the darkest and most fruitless provinces of the intellectual world, a country where every vital impulse was a stranger, a country of Madonnas and bed bugs."

For Teige, Marinetti was undoubtedly the promoter of modern mass activity, but nevertheless he recognized that Marinetti's field was rhetoric.

However, reading his manifestos carefully, you can observe that they contain a healthy revolutionary core, which will prove fruitful for current poetry. He exalts the beauty of the modern world, industrial, technical, urban and capitalist, in a word: he professes Civilism. He disavows plaintive sentimentality but announces it rhetorically, so that he prevents us from entirely believing the sincere tone of his words. [...] He teaches us to measure the value of life by its intensity, not by its duration, to act according to the best of our energies. Marinetti's distrust of the idea and the intellect is in relation to the pragmatist philosophies and Bergson, that precisely define the stillness in the idea, its excessively defined character, its extreme fixity, abstraction and its isolation from reality and the immediate truth, which make it inanimate.[69]

It was clearly difficult for a philo-Marxist such as Teige to accept a discourse that adopted rhetoric and could therefore call to mind an old system used by the policy of opposing belief to confound a substantial need to reconfirm one's own power with words full of meaning. But this was the flaw of interpretation that ideology, be it right or left, attributed outside itself rather than observing its own nature, losing the healthy ability to speak while remaining ready to listen to new sounds.

Part of Marinetti's rhetoric is incontestable and often making his texts heavy going, however it can become selectable with a different all-encompassing eye at work on his private life, his capacity for exportation and dissemination, and the actual results of the Movement in terms of innovation and expressive efficacy.

---

69   Cf. Karel Teige, *Arte e ideologia* (Turin: Einaudi, 1982), p. 101.

CHAPTER II
THE ARTISTIC ACT AS A SOCIAL PROPOSAL: FUTURISM AND THE DOMINATION OF TECHNIQUE

II.1 *Theory of Futurism and Sociological Issues*

Futurism is an anti-cultural, anti-philosophical movement of ideas, intuition, instincts, slaps, purifying and accelerating punches [...] created on 20 February 1909 by a group of brilliant Italian poets and artists.[1] (F. T. Marinetti)

II.1.a *Art as Place of Conflict*

Society is made up of points of union and the relation within it: institutions, communities, and family and the shared reality in terms of values, interests and rituals. How do societies keep together? According to Simmel a society was possible because of the existing relations between individuals, groups and the structure. For Durkheim society was kept together by solidarity, and in modern times it could have survived only if a new type of solidarity was to emerge, which he called organic solidarity. Paraphrasing an analysis by Simmel, this makes one wonder how a contemporary society could be possible, in the sense of community.

In their own context, avant-garde trend can be the evidence of the search for a new type of social cohesion, as an artistic testimony of a reality *à venir*. It appears that the social context at the time could only bring security on the basis of experience.

Experience meant as active builder of history process and a path drawn symbolically from previous and expected experiences. Symbolic thought, which in antiquity was found among oppressed and deeply religious peoples, can be once more found in the multitude of signs produced by contemporary society. The symbolic type of thinking can recap earthly reality and spiritual aspiration, thereby guiding the inhabitant of the new

---

1   Filippo Tommaso Marinetti, *Teoria e invenzione futurista* (Milan: Mondadori, 1968), p. 491.

spatial and mental organization through a reality poised between the social and individual dimensions: the dimension of art and its creation.

Marinetti was the promoter and prophet of this new art-life, but his position included the promulgating of the movement's actions and projects that always left first place to the dissemination of ideas. An initial consideration to be made around the conformation of the movement is that of *pluralism*, both from artistic and theoretical points of view.

The question on the claim of authorship in respect to the Futurist project as the first European avant-garde is hotly disputed, but adherence to the movement was open to anyone who felt they belonged to this "new sensibility".

This is also why the definition of Futurism as a "sect" or an élite can be accepted only by a superficial consideration. In fact, it is far from the real condition of the movement, even because it would affirm a will to stabilization. An easy example of futurist attitude was the extraordinary response to the appeal of the new that was to create an echo such as that of the Frenchman Mac Delmarle who proclaimed himself a Futurist, and also wrote, in turn, in 1913, his *Futurist Manifesto against Montmartre* without ever having met Marinetti: Futurism was a state of mind, an attitude, a way of dealing with history.

To this solitary response from French Futurism, Marinetti could only answer "completely and enthusiastically approved". His message was welcomed and gave fruit, with this action Marinetti's relaunch was to reconfirm the movement as universal and free from nationalist connotations:

> Your brave Futurist initiative shows most clearly that Futurism is neither a *petty religion* nor a *school*, but rather a great movement of intellectual energy and heroism, in which the individual counts for nothing, while the desire to destroy and renew is all.[2]

The existing gap between the claim of Futurism as a movement born from "Italian sensibility" and its ability to interpret the European cultural needs of the moment were not in opposition.

Marinetti's intention was to "reawaken" the Italians, and to involve them in a European context, "deprovincializing" their expectations through the enhancement of expressive, cultural and intuitive qualities oriented to an objective with a more extensive radius, including the adventure of war.

In short, he tried to exploit the vital and intuitive energies that he recognized in the Italian temperament for one collective purpose, less

---

2   *Ibid.*, p. 91.

bourgeois and individualistic than a search for individual peace and a family locked into its daily life.

Futurism was synonymous with "anti-tradition" throughout Europe, with all the consequences that this could have in relation to the institutional organs and those of a traditionalist creed.

In 1913, Marinetti was in Paris with Apollinaire, who "while savouring a delightful goose wrote the Futurist Manifesto *L'Antitradition*, an explicit adherence to the Italian Futurist Movement"[3].

In this Manifesto, which underwent several rehashes and drafts, the Frenchman inserted a list of movements with "futuristic perspectives" such as *"fauvisme, cubisme, expressionnisme, pathétisme, dramatisme, orphisme, fantaisisme, paroxysme"*[4], giving legitimacy of innovation to Futurism as a container of various currents.

Come what may, Marinetti had to accept that its creation would be "relativized"[5] and absorbed by other artistic contexts, but aside from this, his effort was tireless and his figure continued to be conspicuous despite much criticism.

It was in this period, with Mac Delmarle's Manifesto and the words of Apollinaire, that Futurism saw confirmation of its having permanently extended its innovative message, becoming a symbol of an eccentric attitude that strove towards an experimentation that would transcend its exclusively artistic meaning and enter the broadest context of culture.

Because of this same tendency for exchange with other Futurist milieus, in March 1914, Apollinaire received a letter from Léon Bailby, director of the magazine *"L'Intransigéant"*, announcing the end of their professional relationship since, *"vous vous êtes obstiné à ne défendre qu'une école, la plus avancée, avec une partialité et une exclusivisme qui détonnent dans notre journal indépendant, qui nous causent un grand tort moral, et qui ne sont pas sans nous occasionner même un préjudice matériel"*[6].

The indisputably "anti-traditional" significance forced the "traditional" world to take precise sides.

The avant-garde therefore became, in addition to the emblem of a need for a new art, also an example of a different communicative ability of the artistic message. This artistic conception seemed more like a social mission to change the perception and conception of art and the dialectical

---

3   Guillaume Apollinaire, *op. cit.*, p. 10.
4   *Ibid.*, p. 4.
5   Giovanni Lista, *Arte e Politica* (Milan: Multhipla ed., 1980), p. 21.
6   *Ibid.*, p.16.

relationship of art with society, than a need to bring out the use of materials or the most suitable tools to realize this expression.

In this sense, we can associate an idea on the use of art and culture similar to that of contemporary cultural studies which see the cultural terrain as a place for conflict.

Futurism was driven by the desire to revolutionize the world order starting from the stripping of emotions: the overcoming of the sentimental attrition that prevented the action released from the past from creating a mode of action independent from mechanisms linked to materiality.

This movement demonstrated the effectiveness of art as a tool for knowledge, given that the artistic act recognized itself in the clarity of the transformation of reality.

Like science, art has birth from an act of intuition and a revelation of reality: but if science strives to discover the laws of reality through a theoretical and empirical path, art does not depart from nor strive to reach anything, the artistic act presents itself as a witness of reality. The sociological instances, being unable to enter the creative path of the singularity of this act – by definition, inaccessible – can determine the conditions of its origins and the stimuli of change that the artistic act generates both in the society that embraces it, and in the one that rejects it.

An artistic action is the expression of a vision of reality, thus it tends to generate social reactions which trigger the processes of change irrespective of the approval or rejection of the art object. Art can be thought of as the unconscious writing of history.

Artistic theories lead to several dead spots; if we understand art as the manifestation of a truth, we are forced to hope for the return of metaphysics.

On the contrary, art can be made a tool for knowledge (as attempted by the late György Lukàcs), but here the constantly changing dialectic between individual and artistic expression comes into play.

Ultimately, if we abandon the idea of a concept of subjective truth and accept that the aesthetic truth is a clue to the candour of the artist producing it, we risk entering the dialectic of authenticity and rhetoric.

The distiction that Boccioni made between *sincere* and *factitious* artists, the one related to the spiritual nature of art, the other to its worldly dimension, finds confirmation in a progressive doubling of the conception of art.

From a sociological point of view, entering into a relationship with an artistic movement or a work of art cannot bring a question of the work's veracity since it would fall immediately on the specificity and uniqueness of the artistic act[7].

The difficulty of constructing an artistic theory of Futurism was born out of the movement's lack of homogeneity, its internal diversity due to geographical and cultural differences.

The artists' varieties of expression were unified in this movement by the conviction that Futurism meant freedom of artistic expression, that anything could be art if it expressed power and the need for renewal.

With this premise, the foundations of modern aesthetics were laid. Pluralism was the only theory that could contain the sheer variety of Futurism, the same theory that could contain the explosions of modernity.

The social premises of this art can be found in a deep contradiction between an artistic action that was basically disinterested in social and individualistic causes, and was satisfied with a position of quiet marginality from polemical, political and economic implications, and another attitude that was more adherent to the change in the surrounding environment, which translated into a need for active participation.

As a group, the Futurists had organizational needs that were entirely managed by Marinetti, who was both the organizing and driving force.

Among the individual artists who came together to weave the theoretical fabric of the movement through the writing of Manifestos, relationships were tied through friendship and sharing at the Futurist Evenings; basically, the work was individual to be shared at the meetings of demonstration and dissemination.

Futurist activity was split between art and commitment. In Marinetti's writings, we can find various comments on the generous capacity for dedication to the common cause of Palazzeschi, for example, and not of Soffici, who instead seems to have shunned personal exposure as much as possible at public events.

II.1.b *The Dialectic between Societal and Individual Changes*

In Freudian psychoanalysis, the artist is equivalent to an individual who has failed in his or her adaptation to reality, but while in situations of serious illness this disquiet finds no ways of return, for the artist we can talk about *flexibility*, by means of which the individual abstracts from reality, but also knows how to return, possesses the ability to inhabit two parallel worlds, certainly ending up atypical in some of his or her symptoms, but finding

---

7   Cf. Peter Bürger, *La prose de la modernité*, Fr. transl., (Paris : Klincksieck, 1994), p. 57.

deep incentives in the ability to invent an illusory world that fulfils needs unsatisfied by the practical one[8].

The tireless backward-looking gaze, directed mischievously at all the most ridiculous and boring human aspects, was, in the Futurist Reconstruction of the Universe, a continuous paean to inner liberation, potentially extended to all mankind. An inner liberation that used the tools of art.

With the conviction that this creative energy was a potential at the disposal of every individual.

The artists who adhered to Futurism were many, and countless achieved nothing more than a regional dissemination of their art, but it was precisely the movement's newness that demonstrated its innovative power: the unique way in which the new artists saw the world steered them towards new forms and new techniques. The changing environment, both physical and spiritual, opened the road to new thematic materials and therefore required new forms of expression.

The change in the urban landscape was substantial at the beginning of the Twentieth Century, with its dispersion of sensibility through the need for a renewed artistic form. *Il paesaggio e l'estetica futurista della macchina* was a collection of Marinetti's comments on the effect that an aerial view generates on sensibility:

> Second landscape boosted by the eeling of waters and the clouds that mixed, gathered and scattered sparkling towns and woods concentrated like fists of hatred. [...] In a few minutes, three temperatures, three moods, three different landscapes.[9]

The interpenetration of the plans and materials made by Boccioni before 1916 found a concrete verbal explanation in relation to the changed landscape by 1931. The speed of the overlapping images, leaving no time for the sight, moods and physical perceptions to steady, brings life to a fusion of different contexts that converge into a single image: confused, superimposed, and comprehensible only to those who have experienced that same feeling, i.e., only for those who have boarded an aeroplane.

At the same time, the elitist and disseminative dimension appears in these details in all its clarity.

---

8   Cfr. Arnold Hauser, *Le teorie dell'arte,* It. transl., (Turin: Einaudi, 1969-1988) (*Philosophie der Kunstgeschichte*, 1958).

9   Filippo Tommaso Marinetti, *Il paesaggio e l'estetica futurista della macchina, op. cit.*, p. 625.

As someone privileged, Marinetti experienced the dimension which in the future would be a prerogative of everyday life. In 1931, the aerial dimension was shared by those who had the financial means, or by those who had gone to war; there were few other possibilities. The differentiation of sensibility was thus divided in an economic and military sense for those social groups who, by necessity or curiosity, approached this new reality.

The reality was that air transport had not yet become necessary, train travel was efficient and already gave speedy transit times. Culture, if mobile, used the train and the car; the plane was for adventurous souls.

Technology seemed to model the actions of these artists, it directed their interest and attention, leading them to formulate artistic theories based on the new emotions and potentiality developed by this different relationship with the environment.

Desire and the will were obviously affected, and each natural reference was transformed by this event:

> with us begins the kingdom of man with its roots cut, of man multiplied who mixes with iron, feeds on electricity and no longer includes anything other than the sensual pleasure of danger and daily heroism.[10]

The relationship between matter and form was in mutation, which can be seen in Boccioni's studies on movement, his moving sculptures, in formation, mixtures of adjacent objects that merge into one movement, sums of objects impossible to assimilate, yet which between them form complexes that are unique in their movement.

This was a dynamism that created a situation which could be represented by a single object.

"In literature and in study, a tactile sensitivity has existed for a long time. My friend Boccioni, a Futurist painter and sculptor, already felt tactilely when in 1911 he created his study for *Fusion of a Head and a Window* with materials absolutely opposing in terms of weight and tactile value: iron, porcelain, clay and women's hair. This study, he told me, was made not only to be seen but also to be touched"[11].

Experience also meant tactile experience, experience through the senses, and in this direction the movement was the only way to grasp the object in

---

10   Filippo Tommaso Marinetti, *Noi rinneghiamo i nostri maestri simbolisti ultimi amanti della luna, op. cit.,* p. 304.
11   Filippo Tommaso Marinetti, *Tattilismo, op. cit.,* p. 175.

its "pure sensation", in its manifesting to give "the simultaneous form that springs from drama with the environment"[12].

This drama with the environment represented the action of the object in the environment and on the environment, the meaning it took in a dialectic with the outside.

Here too the material was not foregone, but was the bearer of singularity, expression exceeded any question between form and experience, and we can say, in the words of the *Technical Manifesto of Futurist Painting*, was equally valid for plastic materials, where "To paint a figure one should not paint it as something in itself; one needs to make visible its *atmosphere*."

Another crucial point of Futurist expression was the direct action on the public, not only to create a dialectical relationship of reaction, but to move souls, to change the public, change the habit of art, to raise the awareness of the common man to new expressions more appropriate to the current era, in close relation to structural changes.

The first condition for the recognition of a new art was that the public should change expectations, that they should know how to let themselves be transported by the vibrations of a new expression. Futurism reproposed in art what an individual lived through unwittingly in the experience of industrialization, "people, like a car should be studied in their laws of life, i.e. in their dynamism, which is the simultaneous action of their absolute motion and their relative motion"[13].

The speed of cars but also the noise, the smells of factories that mutated olfactory sensitivity, music as noise, life with the rhythm of the locomotive, which, incidentally, in painting was like the *Dynamism of A Dog on a Leash* painted by Balla in 1912.

II.1.c *Organizing Social Action through Analogy and Intuition*

In the exaltation of the analogy, as a rejection of the logical concatenation of thought, the subtle dependency of rationally unexplained acts was sought. The new Futurist man would be free from romantic feelings: "The future man will reduce his heart to its true function as a distributor. The heart must become in some way a kind of stomach of the brain that is filled methodically so that the spirit is able to enter into action"[14].

---

12   Umberto Boccioni, *op. cit.*, p. 86.
13   *Ibid.*, p. 87.
14   Filippo Tommaso Marinetti, *L'uomo moltiplicato e il regno della macchina*, *op. cit.*, p. 300.

Various social studies have promoted the use of analogy as a logical conceptual-empirical tool. From a conceptual point of view, it is usual to consider analogy in its etymological meaning: "a relationship that may exist between the terms of a speech", and it is precisely this *possibility* that can be considered as a method of reason, something that is deemed the usual method in the artistic process.

"Consider possibility as a method of reason, in the sense of believing in a concept of extended and flexible rationality, that uses multiple tools and models"[15]. Analogy is, in the study of social reality, one of the most powerful tools in reducing social complexity, not a superficial process, therefore, but one that brings the complexity of phenomena to a comparable measure.

And this can apply both to phenomenal and conceptual diversity.

Through reduction of the "pleasure principle", the individual would be able to enjoy freedom from social constraints, from sentimentality; with contempt of women working as a symbol for a worn-out version of love: "Love – romantic and voluptuousness obsession – is nothing more than an invention of poets, who gave it to humanity. And it will be the poets who will take it away from humanity, as one withdraws a manuscript from the hands of a publisher who has proved incapable of printing it as intended"[16].

Thus, the individual would draw power and not weakness from the disappearance of sentimentality, and it would be with this new complicity of the individual with the machine that the dissolution of superseded social ties would become possible.

All by means of art.

For the Futurists, the individual might achieve happiness and balance through the dissolution of slavery to sociability which was also a function of sexuality. Through communication, sociability could change, this new bond was not necessarily sociable since it was transmissive, becoming an exchange of formation-information. "The man multiplied whom we dream, will not know the tragedy of old age!"[17] Conceivably would not have time.

In reality, Marinetti adored the new tools and technologies, but did not understand its potential negative evolution, in other words, the perplexity that often accompanied much criticism of the avant-garde was precisely the internal contradiction of this movement that hid a practical immobility in linguistic activism, therefore a critical potential consequence.

---

15   R. Capozzi, *L'uso dell'analogia nelle scienze sociali*, PhD thesis.
16   Filippo Tommaso Marinetti, *Contro l'Amore e il Parlamentarismo*, *op. cit.*, p. 293.
17   Filippo Tommaso Marinetti, *op. cit.*, p. 90.

Moreover, in our own times, old age no longer seems such a tragedy.

In the figurative, Boccioni used every technique to abandon the canons of painting, but not to make "something else"; in the same way, Balla studied movement but did not use other materials that were not the classic ones of the figurative style.

And this is precisely the fundamental point of the apparent contradiction of Futurism: the use of novelty was decanted but did not correspond to actual artistic production.

Yet in their theorizing, everything was extremely clear: trying experiencing the new to create an innovative art that was closer to the common individual, to reintroduce to the public that natural closeness to artistic phenomena which had remained the domain of the elite for too long.

But art must not become something else through this. It must only in a certain way, rediscover itself and its natural function of complementarity to daily life. The praise of the machine can be decoded as an unconditional drive towards the new, whatever represented it: "You should fear everything from the mouldy past. You should expect everything from the Future. Have confidence in progress which is always right, even when it is wrong, because it is movement, life, struggle, hope"[18].

Rediscovering the relationship of art with its own time meant returning to the individual an artistic sensibility that had been divided by awareness of the formation of the subject.

Art fit into this twentieth century context as a new salvation, a possibility of interior change with respect to an outside world that was already perceived as no longer controllable; technological, but too fast and too organized to be able to adapt to a traditional social dimension.

The perception of the world changed, the ability to adapt to it changed, by experiencing the unreal through the collaboration of the machine in daily life, the individual experienced an interior metamorphosis.

In this sense, the use of Marinetti's empathetic analogy unveiled its substantial utility in the selection of information, in the choice of items that could be decisive for a new organization of society, but as regards the construction of a structured organizational plan, a logical quality of the analogy came into play, which organized the movement into a tool to change artistic perception.

Rationality sought a model of explanation or a control mode over the randomness of events and, in the case of earlier art, over the unpredictability

---

18   Filippo Tommaso Marinetti, *Nascita di un'estetica futurista*, *op. cit.*, p. 316.

of creation: "The most powerful tool that reason has produced, or dreamed of, to dominate chance, in order to transform it into a dense causal network, is undoubtedly METHOD. [...] But in the Cartesian *cogito* there is a rebellion, a hi-jacking"[19], and like all rebellions, it would only temporarily resolve the issue of coexistence in the individual and in the nature of order and disorder, art and reason. Moreover, method was only a way of achieving one purpose, repeatable and not strictly dependent on external contingencies.

In the theatre, for example, this attempt at reconciliation and rebuilding was expressed in the need to rethink the scenic space.

Futurist Theatre irrupted into daily life making fun of the audience, even before the show began, and it was the spectators themselves who contributed: "Put glue on some armchairs because the spectator, man or woman, who remains glued will encourage laughter. Sell the same place to ten people: result, obstruction, squabbles, and arguments"[20].

With the far-sightedness to pay for the clothes damaged by the result, so that the joke did not become humiliation; or even to offer free places to characters known for being annoying in order to create spontaneity, surprise, and unforeseen havoc. Indeed, also in theatre the fundamental principles were: Conciseness, Simultaneity, Unreality.

Moreover, the tool of a poet could only be language, action through the word, but certainly not refined virtuosity, which was rejected since it was perceived as rhetorical and mystifying.

At the centre of Marinetti's world was mankind, and it is with this key that all Futurist findings can be read, even the strangest: the man who, inserted in a social reality that was progressively more ordered and controlled, developed the potential for simpler transcendence, from a change in the external world to one in the inner world.

In fact, the founding need of Futurism was to awaken the individual, to open him or her to the economically and politically controlled technical life, to discover freedom in expression lived as action.

The three modes that characterized the concept of Futurism's reality (Conciseness, Simultaneity, and Unreality) were not formed exclusively by the new social condition, they were also a type of perception joined to an extrasensory world of an occultist matrix, which compressed distances in addition to capturing speed; this called into question scientific principles

---

19   Franco Rella, *Metamorfosi* (Milan: Feltrinelli, 1984), p. 33.
20   G. Bartolucci, *Il Gesto Futurista* (Rome: Bulzoni, 1969), p. 20.

such as the impenetrability of bodies[21], staking a claim to the intangible transformational and interpenetrable side (it was with these insights that Boccioni made his sculptures fusing several bodies); reality was internalized, and from external became internal to a perceptual system that was discovering other sensory and cognitive possibilities.

The subject as the centre of perception was the heart of the Futurist reality. This changing visual reality placed the centre in the reaction of the subject in whom rapid impressions of moving objects and the correspondences aroused by memory merged, without reflection.

The art, the strength of the transformation that an action might have on an individual and his or her energies, was invoked and felt by Futurism without regard for the forms actually created, despite knowing that it was the form that recreated the experience to be transmitted through artistic expression.

> Ultimately, there are only two philosophies, one of them accepts life and experience in all its uncertainty, mystery, doubt and semi-knowledge and addresses this experience in itself to deepen and intensify the quality, until fantasy and art are created. [...] There is no expression without joy, without agitation. Yet an inner agitation that is immediately vented in a laugh or a cry, vanishes with its occurrence. Venting is equivalent to ridding, liberating; expressing means to continue in a state, proceed in a development, process the completion. But where there is no administration of objective conditions, and no modelling of materials to realize the excitation, there is no expression.[22]

II.1.d *Critique of Modernism*

The widespread dismay and the rebellion of the cultural environment of manner is understandable, since it had a closing reaction against the experimental or innovative procedures of Futurism, or perhaps it is better to say, cultural diversity, which did not respond to the criteria for identification recognized in consolidated cultural contexts.

It is clear that the novelty of an apparent "cultural" parvenu and loud factotum could not disturb the equilibrium of Italian and European culture, as unstable as it was.

But beyond the uproar that Marinetti had succeeded in making and the contrary uproar with which the criticism was to present it, we can say that

---

21   Ilaria Schiaffini, *Sulla simultaneità nella pittura futurista*, in "Futurismo 1909-1944", Mazzotta catalogue, (Milan: Mazzotta, 2001), p. 90.

22   John Dewey, *L'arte come esperienza*, It. transl., (Florence: La Nuova Italia, 1951), pp. 44-75. .

perhaps it was neither a misrepresentation of the action and word of this social agitator, nor an effective opposition of the message sent. Only that the reception had no tools to capture the action in all its innovative flow.

Marinetti's acumen in using publicity for purposes other than those of advertising had been promptly reversed as pulp fiction: he used the simplest ways to reach all social structures and did so with the most suitable tools for communication, but which generated an opposite effect.

It could not be otherwise, moreover; the ardent proclamations and manifestos of Futurist art were a frontal attack on the indifference and lack of references to understanding the changing reality.

The energy of the Futurists against the environment was often directed towards their own difficulties in adapting to reality, which were transformed into a communicative and expressive art since artistic processing in the tranquillity of the study of art no longer belonged to modernity. And of this the Futurists were aware.

As Aldo Palazzeschi wrote in his *Preface to theory and Futurist Invention:*

> The Preface of my book is composed of a good seventy-five pages of exclusive publicity, without the slightest reference to the poems inside, and thank goodness that it was a book of a certain length, as was normal then; if it had been a book of poetry of today we would have seen a truly original edition since the preface would have made it impossible to add the text.
>
> At that point, Marinetti understood the power of publicity which had to reach the facts and people at all depths and all heights, none excepted, [...] using it for problems of the spirit was considered by conformists as ignominy since no vocabulary possessed a shameful enough word to be able to worthily qualify it.[23]

In fact, through interpretation and revision, every phenomenon took the connotations of what the observer was able and knew how to note, and here too the quality of the researcher could not help but affect the quality of the observation with the margin of necessary, almost desirable subjectivity, to ensure that the social sciences were not among the dead disciplines deprived of precious internal conflicts, which were the seeds of a potential future enrichment.

The observation of society through artistic expression required special lenses.

---

23   Filippo Tommaso Marinetti, *Prefazione, op. cit.*, p. XXI.

By reversing the functionality of art in society from passive to active, Marinetti forcefully reaffirmed all the characteristics of artistic understanding and highlighted the lightness of understanding reality.

Speaking for the first time of the intuitive force that flows from the subject, he introduced the quality that united opposites in a form given by experience, as the first quality of art, from which could be drawn an "intuitive knowledge of matter"; he invented *wireless imagination*, which was supposed to progressively lead to an ever more essential art, increasingly in contact with reality stripped of feeling or the ideological constructions that revolve around it.

Syntax was the intermediary used in the literary field to get the message across; and indeed, in Marinetti's work, which rid itself of the *intermediary* with extreme ease, we find an innovator impulse that turned to the past to destroy any threads of a continuation of tradition.

In reality, to achieve creation of the new needed someone who could open the way to seeing everything that actually belonged to the past, to avoid reproducing it or remaining influenced by it, and this is what Marinetti did in some ways: in his proclamations, he analysed everything to be deleted and with what it was to be replaced, except at that juncture leaving it to posterity, since his role was essentially to indicate art's new social functionality.

And here by "functionality" was meant the role and not the use of the artistic model. Consequently, art could have its active function in modern society through communication; artists were not necessarily communicative, but their trade could only see the light with expressive communication, even if they had the precise awareness and desire not to communicate.

Even negation in art became a tool of communication. In Marinetti, we find the brilliance of communication through modern tools, enthusiasm for the future, the momentum towards the new even before understanding and seeing what the consequences might be.

The artist was different in this way from the intellectual, he dedicated his life but also his body to art, his was a dedication that transcended his own calculation and strategic capacity. "By intuition, we shall beat the apparently irreducible hostilities that separate our human flesh from the metal of the engines"[24].

How could artistic creation be introduced into an organized society that did not recognize anything other than what was functional, and what mode

---

24   *Ibid.*, p. 54.

would this have? The space of creation and diversity became a no-man's-land; whatever could not be used was repudiated.

The avant-garde movements marked the step to a fundamental nub of the socialization of art: the artistic spirit put itself at the disposal of the social cause, it seemed to be history that was making this urgent request. It unveiled its anticipatory potential attempting a rebellion against cultural sensitivity.

It changed the relationship between art and society.

Having grown and developed beyond any expectation, Futurism gathered all the artistic lost souls and without a specific artistic trend, created its identity on the uncertainty of identity, on the lack of references, on the need for experimentation and on the positive strength of innovative hopes.

It overturned uncertainty into creative potential, movement into a study of forms, it left room for the new by turning its back on tradition. The intention was to give form to movement, the growing dynamism of the modern world through painting, writing, sculpture, and music.

The venue was urban life, the squalor of lives cut by efficiency (see Balla's *Polyptych of the Living*), the chaos of the city masses: for the first time, laughter and merriment were at the base of an artistic movement, the representation and even more the experience of a hectic life, detached from the usual rhythms of the body. The body thus began a process of metamorphosis, became the modern battlefield, because this was a physical, sensory understanding, deeper and slower than any mental one.

The relationships between individuals was expedited and changed the sense of depth, the potential of knowledge. The body was the theatre of the struggle, and the pacification of passions and alienations was decomposed and recomposed by all the avant-garde groups; dissected, analysed, fused with other objects, and transformed into a mobile entity. What emerged from it were signs of experience, signs of change.

Futurism expressively filled a contextual social vacuum, like all avant-garde movements. It was the historical fabric that provided the bases for this movement. A new era had begun and they had to invent the way to live it. The experience of art became an instrument to experience life, the action allowed by urban reality was one protected by the "stage" of the city, but in the geographical limitation of a world that was more restricted and at the same time more anonymous and dispersive, in which interaction was minimal.

It is therefore the changing relationship between art and life that is the interesting thing about this movement. More than as an ideology, Futurism must be assessed as poetic. And the character of this poetic is *par excellence* its mobility, its temporariness, availability and exchange, according to a continual vital capacity for renewal, enrichment, and articulation.[25]

The "dizziness of the modern", the ephemeral meetings, the lack of duration in the new dimension of time, generated the abode of the fragment, in whose position the faculty of intelligence could find no references.

The exercising of memory as the basis on which to organize intelligence was the exercising of the body that memorized through sensory experience; therefore, memory was in the body, and it was through experience that this memory could form.

Analogy was already born from experience, Futurism used analogy as an instrument for the liberation of the more unwitting artistic forces, experience was therefore art's point of departure and arrival, and it was precisely this that generated a rebellion of modern rationality in the schemes of the intellect.

"We are the transformers of the earth, our whole existence, the flights and falls of our love, everything enables us for this task (next to which essentially there is no other)"[26].

But the abode of the fragment was only an acceptance of the failure of the synthesis, and not one of its crossroads. Futurism fragmented traditional form, destroyed classicism organized on schemes that were no longer valid in the interpretation of the present, but did not seek the praise of the fragment, in fact fought it: synthetic art meant "combating fragmentarism and introducing the fragment of individuality into a wide synthesis of universal value that might be cosmic."[27], in other words Futurism was recapturing the sense of complexity.

Society was constantly changing, and sociology seemed to be a phase of an actual inner rethinking of its potential to understand the real.

Often, to understand a phenomenon it is sufficient to accept it as such. The issue of research in the social sciences is parallel to the artist's work: what is lacking in current sociology for it to be truly an instrument for observing reality or the dynamics of society? Part of the sociologist's work is observation of society and criticism of its internal inconsistencies; art does not arise otherwise, in expressing reality in a form also the artist recreates another society, a different mode of organization, both social and emotional.

25   G. Bartolucci, *op. cit.*, p. 88.
26   Reiner M. Rilke, *Elegie Duinesi* (Rome: Ed. B.M. Italiane, 1937), p. 95.
27   Maria Goretti, *La Donna e il Futurismo* (Verona: La Scaligera, 1941), p. 88.

The artist, like the sociologist, is an external observer and a participant in social reality, the sociologist observes the laws and the dynamics, trying to make a critique to reduce more apparent imbalances, or even a prophetic gaze may arise with respect to certain phenomena that are highly significant from society's point of view.

The artist is critical but begins with different strings to his bow: art shows what social incongruities create in the individual. The artist gives form to experience, and this too is a criticism but fielded and expressed on an emotional level.

The Futurist artist sought a change in the relationship between art and society. The relationship that was imposed to be obtained in virtue of a communicative liberation, glimpsed by Marinetti in publicity and in a further opening to expressiveness in economics and politics (let us not forget the posters of Mussolini as a Socialist before and as a Fascist later).

Art became the vehicle of action; art was freed from its typical position of powerlessness generated by a relationship with the past, which left no room for growth in the present nor the planning of the future.

> Admiring an old picture is the same as pouring our sensibility into a funerary urn, instead of hurtling it far away in violent spasms of creation and action. Do you, then, wish to waste all your best powers in this eternal and futile worship of the past, from which you emerge fatally exhausted, shrunken, beaten down?[28]

With this new active and interventionist force, artistic intuitions vigorously overcame that of politics and economy, thanks to the strength of communication.

The two problems of interpreting and evaluating modern and contemporary art were born precisely from the Futurist integration of non-artistic tools in the artistic field, and therefore: art as a work of art, and art as communication.

In the first case, there was the risk of an excessive gullibility in the evaluation, isolating the work for its intrinsic value if one considered value as autonomous and independent from the whole economic, social and cultural implication and of the figures of the critic, from production, the art market, and reception; in the second case, a loss of the value of uniqueness and specificity of the artwork with respect to advertising or reproduction in series.

---

28   Filippo Tommaso Marinetti, *Fondazione e Manifesto del Futurismo, op. cit.*, p. 12.

Although the conception of art as communication would aid the relationship with the public by depriving it of solemnity, it also limited its content, forcing it onto the field of action to become an expression of reality.

"Communication, since no longer necessary for an immediate response, smashed the sphere of the concrete daily word, to reach the poetic, imaginative, sacred word"[29].

Art and communication in this sense had something in common: a similar attitude to reality. They launched messages that would be seized in separate ways and would create different answers over time; the historical avant-garde movements had presented these premises.

With the distance of the intellectual, the sociologist changed from criticising to proposing; the artist acted out his or her criticism with the aesthetic form, harmless on an operational social plan, but formative from the point of view of the perception and psychic organization of the observer.

With Futurist art, action married the spiritual necessity of change, in Marinetti the passive resistance of artists found the strength to break through and reveal its own voice. Using tools of communication, but mediated by economic interests.

"Contrary to a famous sentence, revolutions succeed when it is poets and painters that prepare them, if the poets and painters know what their part should be"[30].

II.2 *Futurism and Politics*

The roots of the conditions behind the genesis of Fascism were sunk in an extremely complex historical period.

Much of the historical literature from the early 1900s concentrated its analyses on the origins of the Fascist movement, the transformation from Socialism to National-Socialism to dictatorship, and in these pages can be found a series of cause-effects in conjunction with the totalitarian personality, that of Mussolini, combined with a historical period arguably not ready for a democratic system, i.e., civil responsibility entrusted to the individual.

---

29   Franco Ferrarotti, in *La Lente e lo Specchio*, ed. by Jader Jacobelli (Bari-Rome: Laterza, 1994).

30   Comment by Harold Pintor in Ezio Raimondi, *Le poetiche della modernità* (Milan: Garzanti, 1990), p. 83.

We have seen in historical revisionist studies to what extent the responsibility for creating Fascism was actually a phenomenon to be observed on transpolitical bases: Nietzsche's thinking had already announced a new man, able to transform the individual from the inside and to bring a new order to the question, however this was no dictatorial figure, but a prophecy of a spiritual type.

The bourgeoisie as a middle class between the proletariat and the aristocracy in part represented a summary of democratic society, but within this it lost many gradations that spilled into society in the form of dark forces, phenomena revealed as irrational, since they were not consciously accepted by society.

The Overman no longer handed out the Tables of the Laws along with values to single peoples in restricted epochs, but created "sense" for the Earth as a whole, and for unpredictable epochs: the one who determined values and, by guiding the more sublime natures, steered the course of millennia, was "the Supreme Man".

The most sublime natures were the "Lords of the Earth", the tools of the Overman. Thus, his sovereignty was of a higher variety than any previous kind: it was not gross and immediate, like that of earlier statesmen, nor indirect and bogus, like that of earlier philosophers.

Which is why he could aim at the supreme goal, with his creation: he no longer worked in the material or the pure spirit, but could "operate on man himself as an artist"[31].

Consequently, the "Supreme Man", in this interpretation, was he who could recreate life from the humus of the horrors of humanity itself. The man who passed through fire and with his wounds recreated and transformed himself into a vital new dimension.

The horror of the holocaust became the material and the foundation of the new humanity's very life. The two world wars the prelude of destruction to make room for the new.

Thanks to technology, the social situation at the beginning of the twentieth century saw a rise in middle-class power: few traditions, ambition at work, a social scale featuring money. The middle class became ideal for the proliferation of the new economy based on increases in capital: industry, whether small- or large-scale, formed around feisty personalities who were not so well-read in a humanistic sense; industrial logic demanded decision-making skills and pragmatism.

---

31   Cf. Ernst Nolte, *Il fascismo nella sua epoca. I tre volti del fascismo* (Carnago: ed. Sugarco, 1993), p. 720.

In this respect, albeit not fully aware of their own condition, the lower middle class felt their social instability to a disastrous extent: on one side, the wealthy industrial middle class, on the other, the proletariat with no hope.

The only way out was through an alliance with the fledgling National Socialist party, who protested the rebuilding of the new nation, the new civilization, which appeared to be leaving room for everyone by redistributing wealth and opening up social perspectives, even for those who would have remained excluded by birthright.

The industrial middle class became the antagonistic ally of National Socialism, in sync with the developing party, big business steered clear of political dependence, and thus managed to stay out of danger after the collapse of Fascism.

On the role of the Fascist party in relation to the spread of Futurism, Teige took a precise stance that was different from the usual ones, influenced by reading Prezzolini who, in his criticism of Marinetti's book *Futurism and Fascism* stated that links between Fascism and Futurism essentially dated back to Marinetti's personal friendship with Mussolini.

> However, in reality, Fascism was the antithesis to and a reaction against Futurism rather than an analogy of it. In other words, the exact opposite of Futurism. Fascism glorified the most academic coryphaei of Italian culture. Links between Futurism and Fascism were bivalent, alogical, their meeting totally accidental. And Prezzolini wittily points out that Futurism had established itself more coherently in Bolshevist Russia. The flirt with Fascism caused Futurism considerable difficulties and compromised it. And this was already a symptom of impotence.[32]

He then went on to identify the points which, in his opinion, must fundamentally be granted to the Futurist movement, despite its boisterous way of presenting itself and the vehement but proactive nature of its promoter.

A mere twenty years after the publication of the first Manifesto of Futurism, Teige took stock of the profits and losses of Futurism, concluding that some of its discoveries were factors of enrichment:

> 1) The dynamism of Futurist painting as a precursor of the moving picture, i.e. modern cinematography.
> 2) The typological reform of Marinetti's Words in Freedom as a precursor of modern typographical concepts.

---

32   Karel Teige, *op. cit.*, p. 160.

3) Marinetti's wireless imagination in Words in Freedom as a precursor of the free associations and automatic writing of Surrealism and Poetism.

4) Marinetti's theatrical synthesis as a precursor of current reforms in stage design, the liberation of the theatre, and the attempts to make it less theatrical.

5) Marinetti's Tactilism, poetry to be touched, as a precursor of 'poetry for all the senses'.[33]

According to some interpretations, above all in political sociology, Fascism revealed the presence of a pathological interaction between modernity and backwardness[34].Which might also be considered a potential transformation of modernity.

In fact, modernity, this much-discussed era, failed to find unanimity on the key features of its configuration; its most salient feature arguably the impossibility of being characterized in an exclusive and definitive way. Its characteristic was plurality, hence it was impossible to proceed by characterizations, but the converse, if anything: observing its various manifestations and grasping the link not with institutions, but with the prevailing sources, ferreting out with which world they established themselves.

Studies of Fascism have mostly been evolving based on historiographic analyses rather than with tools of a sociological or socio-political type. In this respect, an effective reconstruction, ostensibly more in line with a rebuilding of the social fabric, is difficult, since part of the reference material is missing, namely, censuses or statistics of a demographic or socio-economic nature.

Was Fascism born out of a sense of disappointment and weariness? The origins of Fascism could be read as a middle-class reaction, starting from the classic bourgeoisie-capitalism syndrome, and yet in some ways Fascism seems to have gone beyond these purely economic/class-conscious dynamics, in fact it brought opposing social classes together and with them, consequential values that not only did not coincide but were even incompatible.

With Fascism, the conservative forces, plutocratic and otherwise, exploited a spiritual orientation that was widespread among not only what is normally called bureaucracy, but the population at large.

---

33   *Ibid.*, p. 164.
34   Marco Revelli, *Italy*, in Detlef Mühlberger, "The Social Basis of European Fascist Movements" (London-New York-Sydney: Croom Helm, 1987).

The establishment of Fascism came about among the ashes of a political regime called Demo-Liberalism; from a regime of relative political freedom, deemed sufficient to guarantee respect for fundamental citizens' rights[35].

And yet those constitutional freedoms and that practice of democracy, as limited as they were, at a certain point proved inadequate and, even worse, were no longer defended, but abandoned.

The practice of democracy is laborious. A democratic regime is necessarily laborious, and implies a civic sense, an awareness of political duty that each individual citizen must uphold.

In a capitalist society, inequality basically depends on an equal distribution of instruments of production, in this way, the institution finds itself crystallizing a regime which from the beginning is structured in the direction of an unbridgeable social gap[36].The difficulty of a democratic balance emerges because of these conditions.

The artistic creations of the early Twentieth Century had an aesthetic relationship with society very different from that of classical art: beauty in the sense of the harmony of an artistic figure vanished, in relation to the needs of the individual and the artist to use expressive means as a protest.

The anger of Majakovskij, the suffering of Artaud, the sarcastic dissatisfaction of Lewis, the surpassing of reality by Breton, the enthusiastic emphasis of Marinetti, could not use an artistic medium with the canons of classical beauty, in this case, beauty was translated in the frequently abstract forms of an abused interiority, a shocked sensitivity, which used artistic means as the expression of a suffering humanity. It had to be shaped in the form of sublime, scaring and fascinating at the same time.

The surplus of the creative forces excluded from the production system found a form in art, a freedom that it granted in the possibility of justification that an existence difficult to standardize could give itself through the instruments of the soul.

In 1913, Majakovskij proclaimed that: "[...] the intensity, the tension of modern life has forcefully emphasized the need for that free play of the cognitive faculties which is none other than Art." But, he continued, already indicating the development of his positions, the subsequent partial renunciation of art as a cognitive faculty, in favour of the art of propaganda:

> This explains the great interest of modern man in art. If the division of labour has generated a specific group of workers in beauty, if, for example, the artist, no longer by painting the 'charm of the *maîtresse ebbre*' is dedicated

---

35   Cfr. Riccardo Bauer, *Alla ricerca della libertà* (Florence: Parenti, 1957), p. 7.
36   Cfr. Paolo Sylos Labini, *Saggio sulle classi sociali* (Bari-Rome: Laterza, 1974), p. 21.

to democratic art, he should say to society in which conditions his work turns from individually necessary into being socially useful.[37]

In this sense, the usefulness of art lay not in its utility, in being *The Other Half* of which Papini spoke: "It is also the kingdom of perfect indifference, the real domain of the useless. Even the evil-doer, for having full right to be called so, must be in some way, disinterested. Only an action without any prospect of utility may be called full, the perfect criminal is the one who only does evil for evil's sake, just as the moral man does good for good's sake and the artist art for art's sake. The absolutely free act, independence from special reasons, i.e. the fact that it is perfectly disinterested, not letting itself be decided by the greatest reason and the most convenient end. Even if we acknowledge that these conditions never occur, the test always remains that men conceive the ideal action, the truly human action, such as that which has no grounds whatsoever outside of itself"[38].

Artists were the "vast proletariat of the genial", who can guide the government through the organization of non-stop theatre, "music will reign over the world, every square will have its great instrumental and vocal orchestra"[39]; Marinetti's poetics and imagination exceeded every reality and contingency, assimilating in his draft any historical, political and social category that attempted a social welfare solution.

The basically positivist and romantic impetus of his conception of the world led him to a "shifted" awareness, in which art arose as the possibility of a filler and a solution to any need.

For Marinetti, the driving force of this exaltation was a conscious search that would find fulfilment in spirituality, but overturn the conception of Christian consolation as a balm for life, in art as "an alcohol of exalting optimism, which deified youth, boosted maturity and refreshed old age. This intellectual art-alcohol must be profuse in all"[40], to arrive at the prophesying of a future in which life would be a *life-work of art*.

Nietzsche's thinking with respect to the attitude of the individual towards history explained and interpreted, perhaps foresaw, many of the actions and theorizations of Futurism.

---

37 Alberto Abruzzese, *Forme estetiche e società di massa* (Padua: Marsilio, 1973), p. 54.
38 Wladimir Majakovskij, in G. Papini, *L'altra metà* (Florence: Vallecchi, 1922), pp. 196-197.
39 Filippo Tommaso Marinetti, *Al di là del comunismo*, in *op. cit.*, p. 485.
40 *Ibid.*, p. 487.

"It is clear how man very often has a need to consider the past in a third way, a critical way; and also of this to serve life. He must have, and from time to time use force to break and dissolve a past in order to live"[41].

We modern men, Nietzsche went on, cannot cope ourselves; only by filling and cramming ourselves with epochs, customs, arts, philosophies, religions and extraneous knowledge can we become something worthy of consideration, i.e. walking encyclopaedias, as we might consider an ancient Greek catapulted into our time.

In 1910, Marinetti published his first novel *Mafarka the Futurist*, in French. The novel was set in Africa, Mafarka wins the struggle against his uncle and becomes King of the city of Tell-el-Kibir. But his aim is higher than that and he aims at creating a new future creature by his own body, with the strength of his own will. The new born is a man-bird that exceeded the natural conditions to raise itself as a liberator and tyrant of the mediocrity of individuals, "contemplate my hardened soul, my agile and vibrant nerves under the implacable shining desire! My metallized brain sees everywhere precise angles in rigid geometric systems..."[42].

In some ways this is already the core of Futurist project: create a man that can be autonomous and free from social and material constraints. A mechanical man in soul and body that slew human weaknesses to be reborn as a Nietzschean Overman. Even if Marinetti was to say that his new man had nothing to do with Nietzsche's superman. A man able to reproduce without the aid of a woman, who generated both himself and his future through desire: "Finally, here I am what I wanted to be; consecrated to suicide and ready to generate the God that each carries in their bowels"[43].

Part of a poem included within this novel will be lately published with the name *Guerra sola igiene del mondo* (War as world hygiene). In this first poem we find already the crucial themes of Marinetti's Futurism: the new heroic man, half mechanical and half human, characterized by a cynical attitude; the warship of war as energy to clean the world from the past; the ambition to a totally new social order; the idea that every epoch should define its own priorities by being driven by young forces and ideas. Absolute trust in the will as the sole component of destiny. The hypertrophy of the 'I'.

---

41   Cfr. Friederich Nietzsche, *Sull'utilità e il danno della storia per la vita* (Milan: Adelphi, 1968/1977), p. 28.

42   Filippo Tommaso Marinetti, *Mafarka il Futurista*, *op. cit.*, pp. 264-265.

43   *Ibid.*, p. 265.

The idea of art as a transfiguration of life in a superior model that transcends the givenness of the present in a society that is complete, working and organized, is the need for interior freedom dictated by the constriction of the individual in modern societies.

Modern man was a "weak personality" according to Nietzsche's thinking, who had already seen the crumbling of the active and militant personality in favour of one educated with the events of the previous centuries, tamed by the wisdom of history.

Having barred all others, the only conceivable way seemed the creation of a new life, an interior life or one of visions of reality in creations that could, through the means of experience, accustom the individual to his personal capacity for self-recreation.

Through artistic partnership, an individual could surrender, to dream, to imagine and to change his or her structures of thought, to turn a vision of reality from negative to positive.

The artistic avant-garde schools acted on this deeply human and universal potentiality, to draw vital forces from the imaginative capacities, from the reorganization of reality beyond its socially organized structures.

And it was for this reason that, in a historical context characterized by an existential chaos like that of the early twentieth century, the words of Futurism enjoyed the premises to be formulated, but did not find a suitable medium to be accepted.

In an essay by Depero we can find a clear awareness that everything they were doing, building and yearning for, could be observed with objectivity only by a man from the year Two Thousand.

As a result, with this hypothetical tour of accusation or judgement, were contrasted the legacies of renowned artists who had, in spite of themselves, the awareness of the importance of their work, even disregarding recognition. The Futurist artists' solicitation for recognition of their artistic value was a request for the "presence of spirit" of the individual in his or her time.

The reaction of the avant-garde was also in relation to the cultural atmosphere of the "Decadents" who preceded the formation of the avant-garde.

The fundamental problem of the modern era seemed to be the militant idea of liberation, of democracy, which, not having yet matured the bases for a society with equal rights, had lost its ability to offer moments of union and sharing, such as rituals, theatre, even grand exhibitions, and the Futurist spectacle itself had no aggregating function, if anything it created havoc. Meanwhile, Catholicism had lost all credibility, even though no appropriate alternative had arrived.

Poggioli, in his recurring alternation of good intuitions, saw that even the blasphemous gesture in the avant-garde was not vulgar, that "its deepest root is sometimes the almost religious aspiration to an emotional and absolute mental freedom, the desire to regain a naivety or an innocence of vision that modern man seems to have forever lost, the eager desire to discover eternal laws of the ideal or perfect form"[44].

The artistic breakdown of the Futurist avant-garde was a cultural break born from a situation of social and intellectual stagnation. The basic terrain had been laid by the revolutionary thinking that had developed since the second half of the nineteenth century from the revolutionary crisis of 1848. In this, Italy was unquestionably the tail end of an intellectual ferment that had formed around ideals of social liberation, especially in France, as the central territorial space of the European continent.

The question was whether this breakdown had been an obvious consequence, a normal evolution of cultural values introduced by industrialization, the Second Empire and the Commune, causing a progressive change in taste and thus also in the perception of art.

In this way, however, we would be unable to explain why avant-garde schools had not arisen in previous historical conditions which, similar from the point of view of revolutionary and cultural changes, such as the London of the Nineteenth Century, and also from the point of view of industrialization and the birth of the metropolis, did not involve such a violent breakdown in values in exploiting art.

While verbally rejecting historical content in the arts, Marinetti put Futurism in a historical and highly contemporary dialectic in his social system, perhaps precisely to emphasize the de-identification with the previous artistic period.

Marinetti's position in this would seem to reveal an extreme subtlety in overcoming the negative and destructive visions of artistic movements among his contemporaries, such as Dadaism, to fight against the actual inability to react to a world that promised to become complex and too fast with respect to the real capacity of the individual.

The many aerial inventions of his poetic art, which would in fact transcend the heaviness of a world of frustrating speed and mechanical performance, struggled against reality through art[45].

---

44   Renato Poggioli, *Teoria dell'arte d'avanguardia* (Bologna: il Mulino, 1962), p. 43.
45   Eberhard Lämmert, Giorgio Cusatelli & Heinz-Georg Held, *Avantgarde, Modernität, Katastrophe. Letteratura, Arte, Scienza fra Germania e Italia nel primo '900* (Florence: Leo S. Olschki, 1996), p. 22.

In Futurist art, it is interesting to note how artistic production was the prelude, which from the dynamism of the figure arrived at destruction in some authors such as Boccioni, but never at actual demonstrations of completely abstract art.

In theatre, with its whirlwind performances shorn of sense, devoid of dialogue, in parts of the *Words in Freedom* of Marinetti and Palazzeschi, the inventor of *Controdolore*, and also in much of Futurist production, it was said that it had produced nothing, but it was precisely this abstraction that left a trail behind it, while the doubt it instilled through these enigmatic presences were exactly the linguistic and expressive material that artistic subjectivity employed: shapes, colours and rhythms, blows, screams and *Words in Freedom* were associations that evaded any project and avoided capture and domination. In this way, submission was blocked, and this seems to be exactly the case of the avant-garde, to regain that otherness which alone led the artist to a dialectic with his time[46].

German Expressionism was also pervaded by catastrophic elements, dominated by apocalyptic visions, strong contrasts, and essential figures. Futurism sprang from an optimistic expectation, like the Vorticism of Wyndham Lewis.

Futurism announced a momentous change that should impact not only the arts, but the whole of society, its morals, customs, even its most private and daily manifestations; however, this change was not an end but a beginning. What the Futurists announced was not a world that was sinking, but a world that was rising. They saw in the end the beginning of the new.

The big city, the metropolis, was one of the quintessential places of industrial civilization and technology: The Expressionists felt it as a privileged place, an expression of a great and positive vital tension. Meidner saw it collapsing, Boccioni saw it growing. For the Futurists, the image of the city was a great bright and colourful amusement park, images that we find with ease on the streets of a good part of the great American metropolises.

Los Angeles, Las Vegas, New York: were they not huge technological and concrete apparatuses embellished with neon signs and buildings that seemed to speak a language in code at the disposal of historical architecture and contemporary art?

So, was Futurism an unrealistic manifesto against the fear of the end? Or maybe great far-sightedness, acute observation of the social situation and its development in the economic and mass entrepreneurial sense?

---

46   Cfr. Eberhard Lämmert, Giorgio Cusatelli & Heinz-Georg Held, *op. cit.*, p. 56.

The other "place", repeated too often, was the machine. And here the same evident difference was reproduced. The Futurists with Marinetti at their head, exalted the machine, theorizing its beauty that stood as an alternative to any human and divine-artistic beauty; Marinetti called the Venus de Milo into question.

If Expressionism and Futurism were both a reaction or anyway a manifestation of the emergence of a technological-industrial civilization, it should be noted that this occurred at various stages of technological-industrial development. Germany lived its years of industrialization in the Seventies and Eighties, Italy instead had its "foundation years" at the time of Giolitti, i.e. in the first decade of the new century.

The dischrony involved differentiation at a cultural level. Germany, for example, by the time Expressionism had been born, had already had the opportunity to "discard" enthusiasm for the new reality, had been able to perceive, beyond the immediate successes, also all the dangers and threats.

Instead, Italy sat at the intersection between the historical avant-garde and the rapid modern development of a country at a time when the latter development was still in its first phase: that of optimistic acceptance and sometimes even fetichistic enthusiasm.

The progressive optimism that the more advanced European cultures had experienced in the artistic medium of Veristic mimesis, in Italy was lived in the medium of dynamism and adoration of the Futurists' speed/machine.

In *Democrazia Futurista*, Marinetti's renovative programme seemed to reproduce in many forms a criticism of history as education of the individual, which burdened the personality of the individual and prevented the natural unfolding of fully living his or her time. The result was, in accordance with Nietzsche's vision, a weak personality, incapable on its own of selecting and observing the constituent values of an individual free to act and choose.

"The Futurist Party wants an Italy that is free and strong, no longer subject to its great past, to the too-beloved sojourner and too-tolerated priests: an Italy beyond protection, an absolute mistress of all her energies reaching towards a great future"[47].

One distinction that must be made, resuming the founding pluralist concept of the movement, is that between Marinetti's personality and Futurism as a movement.

---

47   Cfr. Filippo Tommaso Marinetti, *Teoria e invenzione futurista* (Milan: Mondadori, 1968), p. 349.

We can certainly say that Futurism was Marinetti, but the artists and theorists he loved to surround himself with and with whom he collaborated, may not have been totally assimilated to his thought.

As a movement, without definite rules in the strict sense, Futurism accepted the new, and as such, had a greater openness than other avant-garde movements; however, what we can say is that Futurism contained other movements, despite often not sharing the same ideas on many points.

For example, French Surrealism, when it opted for political commitment, was oriented towards the Third International, Russian Futurism was Bolshevik, Vorticism was substantially apolitical, while Futurism had a less definitive position.

This does seem rather ill-advised since there were statements by Marinetti such as:

> Fascism born from Interventionism and from Futurism, nurtured itself on Futurist principles. Fascism contains and will always contain that block of optimistic, proud, violent, domineering and warrior-like patriotism which we Futurists, the first among the first, preach to the Italian people. That is why we strenuously support Fascism, a firm guarantee of imperial victory in the certain, perhaps proximate, general conflagration.[48]

Futurism had always been assimilated to Fascism given that it became the promoter of the same values proclaimed by the Fascist party.

Marinetti himself became its spokesman, but chronologically the date of birth of Futurism was earlier than that of the National Socialist party and Marinetti expressly declared that he had no sympathy for the Socialists: "This government favoured the Socialists who, waving the Communist flag of a defeated people like the Russians, electorally possessed the Italian people as a tired and happy winner"[49].

The avant-garde as an innovator of language was "genetically" a phenomenon of the progressive type, generally identified with left-wing politics. In reality, the principles that underlay it tended to an evasion of *passatismo* [traditionalism], whatever that might be: "All Futurisms in the world are children of Italian Futurism, created by us twelve years ago in Milan. All Futurist movements are however autonomous. Every people had or still has its *passatismo* to overthrow"[50].

---

48   *Ibid.*, p. 496.
49   Filippo Tommaso Marinetti, *Al di là del comunismo*, *op. cit.*, p. 480.
50   *Ibid.*, p. 481.

For W. Lewis, Futurism was "...a circle or a ballet, and Marinetti's Fascist turnaround is only an opportunistic move, which subordinates the reasons of art to a winning political formula"[51].

There may be some truth in this consideration, but Marinetti had a revolutionary conception of art which he would not relinquish in the name of a political credo. Marinetti's position was that of a revolutionary in art but an ultra-traditional in politics.

Paradoxically, the Fascist policy was the opposite: it wished to be an innovator but favoured traditional art, hence Bottai's policy towards Cultural Heritage.

Ironically, the Italians were more willing to give free rein to Marinetti's belligerence than to his free-word poems[52]. An index that the cultural structures of a little intellectualized country were more rooted, perhaps less aware and therefore more difficult to renew with the lack of dialectic ability.

G. Lista himself spoke of the First National Futurist Congress as an "event prefabricated intentionally to bring political support to Mussolini during the crisis caused by the Matteotti assassination"[53].

However, by '24, Marinetti had already abandoned the conviction of a revolution according to his principles and laid aside the idea of a political Futurism.

History in this case rather assumed the value of a memory that clouded the free choice and action of modern man with respect to a past that was too full, and too long preserved in an aura of impassive perfection.

We are speaking at this jucture of a theoretical history, a history packaged from historical events that neglected history from the bottom up, the history of individual life as an invisible corpuscle which, in number, goes to form the history of mankind. "Cicero already had in mind a thought of this kind, when he called it *vita memoriae*. Its legitimacy is based on the fact that human passions do not let themselves be controlled by the general precepts of reason"[54].

Futurism was a movement with a deep sense of history, so much so that it could present itself historically as another consciousness, as ways of living, feeling and fulfilling others.

It is common sense to speak of Futurism as an ahistorical movement, absolute, devoid of historical consciousness only because the necessary

---

51   Maurizio Serra, *Al di là della decadenza* (Bologna: il Mulino, 1994), p. 137.

52   Giovanni Lista, *Arte e politica* (Milan: Multipla ed., 1980), p. 60.

53   *Ibid.*, p. 18.

54   Cf. Hans Georg Gadamer, *Verità e Metodo*, vol. I, (Milan: Bompiani, 1996), p. 20.

radical contrast of the movement in all its statements and actions openly desired to be ahistorical, but was not.

Futurism was profoundly historical in all of its production, because it was in a continual dialectic with the past, and this would seem precisely the motivation of an impossible projection into the future.

The necessary deconstruction of the past, the demolition of old customs anchored Futurist production to its "enemy", leaving the movement without an identity if this failed. Evoking the errors of the past served to demolish it, but in itself this was also a work of continuous re-evocation.

From here there was no escape, Futurism became an essential movement for the future, but in itself was stuck in the past, a bridge that could not be detached from the shores it linked. And this bridge was a passage or a place of transit that served to see what was being left behind and what the future held.

In its formulation, Futurism contained the essence of virtual change, the prismatic and multiple affectivity of modern man, quick and essential sexuality, a passion for speed and transformation as necessary conditions of the modern individual.

Thinking became unconscious, it thought in images with a rapidity that only associations of the Spirit could afford.

It seems that we can find in the Futurist ardour a chaotic disclosure of the love of the individual, an absolute faith in the absence of the concept as a structure which burdened and tried to bend the multiplicity of the real to the limitations of the intellect.

What reality shows us finds, in intellectual and philosophical explanation, only a part of the truth, the rest is inaccessible to us with the tools we have, while, through art, the spirit frees itself, seeks no explanations for itself, lives the present as a reality interpreted and transformed by the filter of the human senses, plus something inexplicable but concrete, like that utopian leap which always allows us to leave a space of imagination and creativity between what we live and know how to explain, and what is impalpable but indispensable in it.

In its inaccessibility, the Futurist artistic method was highly comprehensive of the changing reality of the early Twentieth Century.

What in everyday life was alienation because not comprised by rational awareness, found its place in Futurist expression.

The crankiness of Balla in observing the movement of the dog, the voracity of Depero in the use of any material, the very frenzy of Marinetti for verbal communication, found their statute in Futurism, identification in a movement that had no precedent, with its ability to *understand* the reality in transformation with greater generosity

CHAPTER III
AN AUTHORITARIAN ACTION:
THE HISTORICAL TIES OF FUTURISM

III.1 *The Premises of a New Social Order*

The education of individuals for satisfactory social integration is essentially cultural, including the learning of behaviour and the conventions shared and encoded by society.

The cultural nature of the individual enables reproduction of society through established cultural norms, if we consider culture as a tool built by mankind to make moves and reinvent the historical/social context inherited from previous generations, we cannot avoid considering its change as being inherent to its function.

In this sense, a further clarification must be made in relation to which aspect of culture is being observed, since also the definitions vary depending on whether the emphasis is on the *subjective* dimension (the presence of values, behaviour patterns, interiorized normative criteria, ways of thinking); or on the *objective* nature of the forms of culture (collective memory, tradition accumulated over time and codified)[1].

With changing conditions of interaction with the social context, the cultural tool to adapt to the new conditions changes its statute.

For Simmel, culture is born "when two elements meet, neither of which contains it"[2]. The two elements of the subjective soul and the objective spiritual product, comprising in objective spiritual products all forms such as art, customs, technology, science, social standards, the Law, institutions, in a path of stages that the Spirit must travel to conquer its own particular value, its culture.

The subversion of the traditional social order then takes place in the undergrowth of innovative cultural practices and those that are born from the union of two or more layers of culture, hybridizations, or the use of old

---

1   Franco Crespi, *Manuale di sociologia della cultura*, (Bari-Rome: Laterza, 1996), p. 4.
2   G. Simmel, *op. cit.*

tools in new contexts, and vice versa. In the adaptation of communication to contemporary languages using the tools at its disposal.

Through this objective approach of contemporaneity, the individual progressively becomes accustomed, perhaps even uncritically, to the new reality that surrounds him or her, and starts to use it.

As an artistic movement, hence a promoter of taste and a new aesthetic, Futurism rebelled against a unique reality, sought the multiplicity of the real, since this is what it lived off: the perfection of the machine, the view from an aeroplane in flight, the multiple rounds of the machine gun, the speed of trains and mediated communication, the film maker who accelerated the timeframe of daily scenes, the theatrical scene that became a summary of impressions.

These were all elements that burst into tradition multiplying the points of observation of reality and with this reality seemed to multiply in turn. Remaining firmly in an awareness of the fragility of the new, the explosive artists of the future knew they had no present, and proceeded by trial and error, albeit triumphantly.

This was one of the major contradictions of the movement:

> We were the first to declare the need for us, artists immersed in the chaos of an age-old era that is breaking up and already partakes of the vibrations of a new era being born, to advance continuously, to surpass ourselves without respite, never settling on our laurels, attributing to each of our works the fleeting value of an attempt, of an investigation in the void to be explored, a step towards a marvellous distant synthesis to be reached who knows when.[3]

Reality became a prism because it was analysed in all its movements, the action was broken up into fragments, like the flat sequence of a cinema film, fast but unilateral, multiple because sectioned.

Marinetti gathered and contacted the most eclectic and impetuous people of Italian art in the early Twentieth Century, which is why the distinctive characteristic of the group was dictated by some of its great masters: Balla, Boccioni, Depero, Balilla Pratella, Russolo, Fillia and Sant'Elia in architecture, who were distinguished for their common artistic activity, but developed personality and ways of composition that intersected at certain moments, to then develop into works with a strong personal character.

The group had a strong corporate component, Marinetti contributed letters, encouragement, criticism and affection to all the artists in turn, looked after the publishing of their works, ensuring they were paid by

---

3   Emilio Settimelli, *Inchieste sulla vita italiana*, Rocca S. Casciano 1919.

publishers, organizing Futurist evenings, but with no discrimination over their work: Futurism meant movement, tension towards the contemporary, tension towards change.

In the search for autonomy of creation, Futurism implemented that modern operation of release from a unidirectional dependency, Futurist art did not exclude any expression from its experiences: advertising, tailoring, interior design, illuminated signs for the city, music, theatre, photography, literature, and plastic compositions.

The Futurist movement entered into contact with every creative situation of its era, probed all the expressive and communicative possibilities. Marinetti was the first to use hype through the strategy of the manifesto and this search for autonomy from a single contact, the artwork, with the referent exploiter of art, and in turn the critical and learned circle around the work, shifted the potential dialogue from elitist to universalized.

The actions and theorizations of Futurism triggered that intolerance for the stability of forms, for the persistent existence of the artwork as an expressive seal of a shared social concept, as a representative scheme of a historical era at the peak of evolution; in this case Simmel said that it was possible, in those times, only to obtain a behaviour that was socially positive from social standards, and from the arts only a sterile enjoyment, as fixed offshoots of a formal cultural structure.

From this point of view, Futurism's initial operation confirmed the belief that it was the historical period which stimulated a change in artistic expression, and consequently the social codes shared through taste. However, one of the key values of the reconstruction of the Futurist universe proposed synthesis as the fundamental quality of the new era to orientate itself in the constant movement. And here was an unintended response in the work of Simmel who, with a sharp criticism of the modern world's facility to progress through synthesis, illuminated one of the most elementary oversights of the movement.

> Only a time tending to analysis like the modern era could find the greatest depth, unity and totality in the formal relationship of the spirit with the world of synthesis. On the contrary, there is an original unity that precedes any differentiation. [...] Creative genius possesses that original unity of the subjective and objective elements, which to be reborn in a completely different form, in a synthesis, in the process of acquiring culture by individuals, must first unfold.[4]

---

4   Georg Simmel, *op. cit.*, p. 94.

The exemplification of a creative process in which there was uncertain progress by trial and error, typical of artistic intuition and an as-yet undefined expression of a change that was not complete. Moreover, adopting a language meant creating a world and defining its rules. A further concept developed by Simmel that might prove useful to us in illuminating the path of this artistic phenomenon, is the essential independence of culture from the objective meanings of a work.

This observation, published around 1911-12, showed the need to enter into communication with the expressions of the epoch, an awareness that the incomprehensibility of contingent time could bring life to an artistic tendency which led, through the need to survive, to denying the present as the result of a past, in order to turn towards a future indicated by the way of independence and subjectivity as the birthplace of the objective. However, this did not leave a representation of the real, but an expression of the contingent.

The very choice of the means of propaganda for the Manifesto, the newspaper *Le Figaro*, indicated the message: "a press campaign" in the modern sense, with well recognizable elements: speed and dynamism, striking headlines, news content. The modelling of the daily newspaper as a communicative language was the first in a long series of which the structure of Futurist language was composed"[5].

In this way, increasing the listening and visual potential, increased the relational dependence on the outside, which, from an elitist fruition became more widespread.

What was it that happened in this operation involving social synthesis, but that did not necessarily guide understanding? The shared experience of the work of art that assumed a predisposition to aesthetic taste or at least to aesthetic fruition, became a more emancipated time but also one that was more dependent on society.

The complexity of the decoding, generated by the vastness of the reception of the message in more heterogeneous contexts, added a further margin of misunderstanding to the already complex character of the Futurist movement.

The fact that it presented itself as an artistic group who immediately used means not traditionally intended for the dissemination of art, immediately created a mixed hybrid image that could not be pigeonholed as a unique genre.

---

5   Lorenzo Taiuti, *Arte e media,* (Genoa: Costa & Nolan, 1996), p. 26.

E. Morin indicated self-organization as one of the two basic concepts of modernity, together with complexity. Complexity, understood as an organized and unique system formed by a set of features that made up a unitary system, could not be considered separately from the concept of self-organization.

The example that *Le Paradigme Perdu* brought was a perception of reality based on its smallest units: the discovery of the cell, the basic unit of life, organized as an inseparable but at the same time complex system in that it is rich in functions necessary for its own life, perceptively reorganized human life based on unique complex systems, that were monadic, self-sufficient, but interdependent, and the more uniqueness and self-sufficiency increased, the greater the dependence on the outside, as a functional unit forming part of a system.

The conceptual nub was precisely this: self-contained but dependent systems. Units highly organized internally, but that participated in the achievement of a suprapersonal balance. Related monads, which only appeared as such in interrelationship, precisely because they were self-organized. And this would also seem to be the scheme of linkages in contemporary society.

In addition, a constituent element of Futurist experimentation based its theoretical outbursts on an acute observation of the changes in reality: in this regard, Boccioni, in his theoretical writings on Futurist painting and sculpture spoke of a new emerging instinct which the avant-garde artists should be aware of: "The instinct of the complex", "we grasp EVERYTHING through the complex while those of the past gathered LITTLE through the simple. And finally, everything is easy when it is life or intuition"[6]!

Intuition, the duration of the movement that brings dignity to an object in relation to the environment, the new mechanical individuality, the exasperation of "spiritual speed", the sense of the public as a monster created by the collective dimension, the idea of being able to divide artists into two categories, that of the *sincere* and that of the *artificial*, one scholars of the nature of art, the other scholars of art in the worldly dimension, were all expressions of a cognitive and critical process of the cultural situation in Italy.

The Futurist movement drew its artistic laws from the new certainties of science, was guided by the sensitivity exasperated by the new conditions of life, tried to bring dignity of form to the "emotionally deformed".

---

6   Umberto Boccioni, *Pittura e scultura futuriste* (Milan: SE, 1997), p. 21.

"We Italians need the barbarous to renew ourselves, more than any other people, because our past is the greatest in the world and therefore the most formidable for our own life"[7]!

Innovating meant forgetting the past, teaching the Italians love for research, to overcome their natural tendency to compromises, advancing into the contradictions of the creative process, "against Cubism, whose bases were and are static and indifferent, i.e. indifference and denial of subject-emotion"[8].

Certainly, the contradiction is evident when it passes from exaltation of the new mechanical individuality in search of "subject emotion", a contradiction of modernity.

Morin continued:

> C'est à Schrödinger, un des pionniers de la révolution biologique, que nous devons l'idée capitale que l'être vivant ne se nourrit pas seulement d'énergie, mais aussi d'entropie négative, c'est-à-dire d'organisation complexe et d'information.[9]

The individual was considered an open system, who entered into a relationship of integration with the outside where the constitutive identity was generated from the inside by its system of self-organization, which was also self-creative regeneration that made itself communication towards the exterior of an experiential reality. The more autonomous the living system was, the more it depended on the ecosystem, Morin said, glimpsing the deep complexity of the autonomy which to be such, fed off a great wealth of interrelationships.

In this same vein, we have spoken of complexity and the self-organization of the individual, of culture which, step by step, integrated the growth of the individual and the social context; the work of art, like any other product of human expression, became a bearer of the values of the order to which it referred, both in its version of adaptation to or subversion of that order.

This was a sphere of culture that included several realities, interior, socialized, and contradictory:

> feelings, emotions, the dimensions of desire and of the individual and collective imagination, representations of natural and social reality, conceptions of the world and life. Art is becoming increasingly autonomous as a complex

---

7   Boccioni, *op. cit.*, p. 81.
8   *Ibid.*, p. 83.
9   Edgar Morin, *Le paradigme perdu: la nature humaine* (Paris: Seuil, 1973), p. 31.

set of forms of symbolic mediation, drawing its inspiration from the most varied types of experience.[10]

The phenomenon of Futurism proclaimed elements that would constitute the parts of this new social order. It brought form to an artistic group equipped with theoretical bases that were not erudite but experiential.

In the naivety of its idolatry of the machine, however, in addition to the maximum freedom of the individual from his or her "traditionalist soup", it was unable to foresee that the use of technology as a division and selection of competencies created on the one hand a levelling of traditional hierarchy, and on the other, a new situation: a hierarchy of skills which, having achieved the experience of action in contact with the machine, led to a gradual disappearance of the place of experience that is decisive for the sense of unity and sharing among individuals, but also the integrity of the individual within it in the formation stage.

> For the first time in history, the possibility for the individual to enter a relationship with other individuals was determined, thus 'creating society', without this implying any link of a personal nature [...] individuals react to the sense of impotence they experience by falling back on themselves, and, with the impossibility of recognizing themselves communally, end up considering society itself in purely instrumental terms.[11]

The need was evident for an expanded consciousness, a psyche adapted to the changing social system, broader, globalized, generalized, and depersonalizing.

The globalization phenomenon could be reduced to human dimensions only through small groups and multiple relationships. The family nucleus remained necessary for its sense of belonging, but in contemporary society, the opening of group membership extended not only to the ties of kinship but also the belonging of identity.

The basis of forming identity, which was originally down to the family, now seemed to create its humus from more peripheral ground: from tastes, aspirations, and motivation.

The foundation of the culture of the fragment.

The formation of the individual increasingly took place through institutions or information networks, rather than direct interaction with the

---

10   F. Crespi, *op. cit.*, p. 180.
11   Umberto Galimberti, *Psiche e techné. L'uomo nell'età della tecnica* (Milan: Feltrinelli, 1999), p. 44.

family nucleus. Now more than ever, individuals seemed to be defined by the choices they made, and yet, it would seem, their tools for a faculty of conscious choice were drastically reduced.

The foundations of identity were often dangerously precarious. There were possibilities to choose from, but there was no suitable culture to use these possibilities, to learn to understand the consequences. Membership became similarity, but culture in the broadest sense was such when it varied in its aspects and nuances.

Mankind, as a cultural being, began, through cultural revolutions, those slow changes in perception and thought that led to the transformation of society and its organization.

The organization of the structure of social communication passed through this fragmentation of shared reality, and made communication itself freer, leaving room "...for experiments in and between languages, for changes of paradigms, in the hypothesis of a communicational metropolis in the face of social dissipation"[12].

The Futurist movement was one of these.

The *Futurist Reconstruction of the Universe*, the Manifesto signed by Balla and Depero on 11 March 1915, was a three-page declaration of the total new art.

The recognition on several occasions and in several manifestos of the necessity that every single artistic skill went to form a unit with the artistic corpus of creation.

Just as the universe comprises every manifestation of life in all its forms, so the Futurist reconstruction of the universe laid the foundations of a total art, an interpenetration and overlapping of limbs which only together found the completeness and complexity of creation.

> We Futurists, Balla and Depero, wish to achieve this total fusion to reconstruct the universe while energizing it, i.e. recreating it totally. We will give the skeleton and flesh to the invisible, impalpable, imponderable, imperceptible. We will find the abstract equivalent of all the forms and elements of the universe, then combine them according to the whims of our inspiration, to form plastic complexes that we will set in motion.[13]

---

12   Massimo Canevacci, *Culture extreme* (Rome: Meltemi, 1999), p. 49.
13   Fortunato Depero, Quaderno n. 14, MART, Archivio Storico, Fondo Depero, ms. 3822.

Understandable and decodable from a broader perception, freed from structural conventions to come together on an "electric" and sensible plane of perception. Almost tactile.

The centrality that subjective reality acquired in the context of a sociological study through artistic work, drew attention to the potential of transformation that it produced in the individual.

What Berger and Luckmann indicated as "restructuring", that phenomenon which required "processes of re-socializing that resemble primary socialization, because they need to radically redistribute the values of reality and then reproduce to a considerable extent the strongly affective identification that joined the individual with the familiar environment"[14], was like the dialectic procedure through which artistic creation affected the construction of individual reality.

Language is a way of ordering reality and creating a world, so we can say that "restructuring implies a reorganization of the apparatus of conversation", i.e. the language of the code, which can be artistic as well as verbal. We can speak of the Futurist reconstruction of the Universe in terms of "restructuring" of the linguistic, behavioural-social imagery of reality, a total art presented as a tool of social "conversion".

The original structure of conversion was the religious one, which, more than providing "conversion", proposed the potential for the maintenance of this change in radical values. Conversion could be maintained and reaffirm its status only through a support structure that it reconfirmed in new values: in the case of religion, the religious community, but in lay spheres, we could say the same of political indoctrination and psychotherapy. In the artistic field, this environment was superseded by complicity and the common idea of realizing a cultural renewal project.

All of this happened through the crushing of the old linguistic-artistic codes and with the reorganization of conversation. As in fact occurred in the context of Futurist reconstruction: "Balla and Depero move within a more global dimension, which announces the new times and involves varied and numerous interests, connecting and unifying them all in an aesthetic desire for a total intervention of transformation"[15].

Through the medium of art, the universe was entirely rebuilt, by means of imagination, colours, and plastic materials: "metal wires, cotton, wool,

14   Peter L. Berger, Thomas Luckmann, *The Social Construction of Reality: A treatise in the sociology of knowledge* (New York: Random House, 1966), p. 182.
15   Maria Drudi Gambillo, Teresa Fiori (ed.), *Archivi del Futurismo*, voll. I-II (Rome: De Luca, 1962).

silk, of any thickness, coloured. Coloured glass, tracing paper, celluloid, metal mesh, transparencies of all kinds, colourful fabrics, mirrors, metal foils, coloured foils, and all the very gaudiest substances. Mechanical and electrical appliances; musical and noise-making devices; chemically brightened liquids of variable colouring; springs; levers; pipes, etc."[16].

Art lived, through the recreation of reality, in one of the various orders of which Schütz speaks regarding multiple realities[17], each with its own specific and distinct way of "another" existence with respect to the daily dimension.

The creation of Futurism found its identity in relation to the object-machine of the artistic subject, while cultural references from the classical artistic tradition were communicated in the negative. And by "daily dimension" was meant a mode shared by the masses, while the daily dimension of the artist was linked to creation, to the time of the conception and realization of a work, clashing with a very practical everyday life but of a different nature than the organized life of social production.

The artistic dimension was created and re-created in a protected microcosm made up of external events, filtered and altered perceptions that defined reality with organizational bases different from the practical ones of daily life.

In the study of Futurism, therefore, we can only find our way if we assume that the new world imagined and created by this movement was in relation to its principles.

Futurism created a dimension of artistic life that revealed its underlying principles through its Manifestos.

And these same values were merely the summary in art of the technical changes that occurred in the first decades of the Twentieth Century, relating to the contemporary rhythms of life.

It was the new subjects that showed the artist the new plastic sense, the new style, the appearance of new forms, more vibrant, more clashing, more chaotic, and more nervous, which must necessarily lead to a change in the modes of expression[18].

Futurism assumed the values of modernity and placed them at the foundation of its artistic action: in *Pesi, misure e prezzi del genio artistico*, Bruno Corra and Emilio Settimelli wrote in the 1914 Manifesto: "A unique concept of evaluating a work is the value determined by the necessary

16   G. Balla, F. Depero, *La ricostruzione futurista dell'universo*, 11 March 1915.
17   Alfred Schütz, *Saggi Sociologici* (Turin: UTET, 1979), p. 181.
18   A. Soffici, *Il soggetto nella pittura futurista*, in "Lacerba", 1 January 1914.

rarity, and the necessary rarity of a creation is in direct proportion to the amount of energy required to produce it."

For the first time, art was spoken of as an "exactly measurable cerebral secretion", the use of renewable energies in the brain being dictated by the diversity of elements that blended creatively in a work; in this way, the analogue creative coupling of objects not assimilable to one another was incited. In this way, Boccioni created the first plastic creations of objects in fusion with organic material: parts of the human body with objects.

The work of art assumed a value in relation to the environment in which it was created, artistic creation opened up and impinged on the non-artistic world: "The kind of work can acquire a value because of the conditions of the environment in which it is produced: its polemic value, of abstraction"[19].

The difficulty in understanding the Futurist movement is precisely this: to be able to grasp that the validity and purpose of these artists was to leave behind not a work of art or a history of Futurism – as part of a history of artistic evolution – but a liberation from the constraint of art as a product of mankind. A conception of art as an expression of the relationship with time and its organization by an individual dominated by his or her era.

In this way, an artist of a different type was delineated: not the superior individual inspired by divine resonances, but a more perceptually open individual who responded with an immediate creation to stimuli from the surrounding society. The path of the new artists was targeted to respond in a timely manner with works of art to rapid incomplete stimuli that the machine aroused in their nervous system.

And this work could only be the result of an action of synthesizing the real. Where by "synthesising" is meant the "selected" assimilation of the best of the immediately preceding artistic movements: Impressionism and Cubism.

From Impressionism was learnt the deformation of bodies through the light of the environment with its forms created in relation to the vibrations of light; instead, from Cubism, what changed was the breakdown of figures to discover their uniqueness and essentiality, to the detriment of movement which was not perceived in a relationship with an exterior. Staticity was the point of departure of Cubism.

The Futurist current arose as a moment of synthesis between the deformation of the object depending on the light and the description of movement – not according to a fragmentation of the planes of light – but by interrelating the object with external reality. For this reason, Futurist

---

19   Bruno Corra, Emilio Settimelli, *Pesi Misure e prezzi del genio artistico*, 1914.

theory did not recognize itself in traditional artistic theory, since it assumed the artistic object from a point of view that interacted with the surrounding situation.

Plastic dynamism was born, which was closely related to the plastic humour of the individual artist. For this reason, reality, while being the same for all, was never perceived nor portrayed by all in the same way. The prism through which everyone observed reality was given by the human faculty and was therefore unique for each individual.

Futurist art achieved maximum expression when it was the artist's expressive power that decided the mode of expression and not the artistic current that channelled artistic enthusiasm into an already known language.

The avant-garde schools generated a renewed conception of the role of art in society. The new reality awakened artistic practice and showed its close interdependence with social events and especially with the resonance that they produced in the links with the individual and collective fabrics on a psychological plane. We are not speaking here of the collective imagination. Nor commonplace sensibility, but something more profound; there was a deeper investigation of the motivational instincts that were actually extraneous to the awareness of action but that affected its direction.

In other words, it was assumed that art, and especially the art-in-life of the Twentieth Century avant-garde was an engine of psychological activation, almost a rite of passage preparatory to the world of contemporary technology: a means of orientation for the individual to adapt to society.

The speed of the new world, the distraction of the many stimuli, demanded a strong-willed affirmative art, able to impose its presence by leaving in the mind of the spectator a seed of curiosity, or intuitive attraction; this goal could not be achieved through the traditional performance of the arts. For the first time, the artistic process recognized itself in an object, or in a social function.

Theatre found itself having to compete with cinema, and therefore had to speed up its performances, make them more in tune with a reality that experienced everything at the same moment: actions, sounds, movements, music. The new theatre was one of variety, a theatre of contamination, which made no distinction between the various arts of movement and music to grab the spectator's attention. Concentration had to be continuously *stolen* through a forced return of attention, whether the stimuli were colour, music, dance, or movement. Even though in the chaos of this free admixture of all possible expressive tools, this type of art aimed at uniqueness, a restoration of the unification of the experience in an apparent lack of the organic in reality.

Marinetti listed the "modifiers" of modern sensibility that created significant phenomena, and from which new values derived:

1. Acceleration of life, which today has a fast pace. A physical, intellectual and sentimental balancing act on the tensioned cord of speed between contradictory magnetic poles. Multiple and simultaneous consciousnesses in the same individual. (Speed, Dynamism)
2. The horror of what is old and known. Love of the new, the unexpected. (Novelty)
3. Horror of the quiet life, love of danger and a yearning for daily heroism. (Heroism)
4. Distribution of the sense of the beyond and increased value of the individual who wishes to *vivre sa vie* in line with Bonnot's phrase. (Autonomy)
5. Multiplication and confinement of human ambitions and desires. (Multiplicity)
6. Exact knowledge of everything that everyone has that is inaccessible and impractical. (Sense of Limit)
7. The semi-equality of man and woman and less difference in the level of social rights. (Media Democracy).[20]

Speed and dynamism were the immediate consequences of the changed social conditions; the awareness of these new bases which future modernity would rise from was the centre of Futurist production.

While the late nineteenth century had seen awareness of the emergence of new social subjects and, with them, novel issues linked to a more indirect exploitation of work through interaction with the machine, and the Marxist question of the alienation of the individual and the impersonality of industrial labour, also in art there had been a rapid succession of artistic modes of representing reality that belied and overlapped each other in search of an expression of the new or different.

In Divisionism with Segantini, Pelizza da Volpedo, and Medardo Rosso in sculpture (although he cannot be numbered among the Divisionists), a social change can be observed trying to transpose the new reality through new methods of representation, by decomposing the reality that they seemed to be decomposing into.

Hence, with the perceptual rigidity of the classical period that art needed as a reproduction of reality, Futurism took a leap, and with this, the need for violence to break the continuity with the past is understandable.

---

20   Filippo Tommaso Marinetti, *Noi Futuristi* (Milan: Quinteri ed., 1917), p. 10.

For the Divisionists, reality was decomposed, the speed and diversity of social situations confused the image and broke it up into its most minute particles.

Divisionism focused on the destructive reality of the new sensibility; like survivors among the rubble trying to analyse what had happened.

Futurism instead made the effort to leap into the void, it perceived that the core of the new social sensibility would be given by adapting to the speed demanded by technology, this was a movement exalted infantilely as "of the utopia of progress" but was also aware in its depths that all of this would lead to a substantial precariousness.

Boccioni's momentum of interpretation in painting the "three women": his mother, his sister and the woman with whom he had an intense tormented relationship, with the lines of strong colours that run along the garments of the subjects are together the transmission of contradictory signals.

The three subjects belong to the affective sphere, show attachment to their own emotional identity, but at the same time are disturbed by the movement of sharp colours inside them: cool tones that stray across the real plane of the clothes are a part of them but join them to the rest of the image, which seems to have multiple plans. The choice of the subjects belongs to classical family portraiture, but only where the intimacy of the affections is crossed by tones that predict the impersonality of movement and prepare a subsequent full-blown involvement of the artist in the whirl of nervous stimuli of the metropolitan condition.

The portrayal of reality was not only an image of facts, but above all an expression of the processes, potential and motivational energy that led to an explosive expression. Explosive since not recognized and especially covered and repressed by industrial civilization. Which is why the subject of the Futurist was movement and moods; all the social phenomena caught in their evolution.

The importance of the introduction of the machine into daily life lay in the speeding up of production and movement, and the modes of expression to communicate this new dialectic relationship of the individual were embodied by two distinct forms: a dialectic with the animate and another with the inanimate, with technology.

The interpretative and perceptual leap was also reflected in those abstract perceptions that had been previously neglected by artistic production, neglected in the sense that no need had been felt to make them visible.

Futurism (but earlier also Impressionism with its display of vibrations, Pointillism with the fragmentation of the image into its smallest unit, and Cubism with the prismatic nature of the image and figures) – as I was saying – made a synthesis of the explosion of the visual and the perceptual, giving rise to a free expression of creative energy; the importance of the work was revealed by the power of expression, not the figurative result or, better, the figurative result *was* the artistic power.

The strength of Futurism, like that of its works, lay in its ability of dissuasion from an artistic habit to an opening towards the dynamic state of art as a life lived to the full. Often, what remained was not the work of art, but the change it had been able to impose.

On a social plane, what did the change in perception from the habit of a beautiful art, to an art that was strong and expressed power bring? The art of Caravaggio is also powerful, it consists of strong contrasts and symbolic chiaroscuro, but the outcome is completely different. Futurist art expressed the desire to be a force in a time of extreme weakness for humanity, tried by war on the one hand and by increasing bureaucratization on the other, but by reaction became its ally.

The colourful constructions of Depero, the words-in-freedom of Marinetti, the *Intonarumori* of Russolo, the fusions of organic and inorganic materials of Boccioni, were the astonished answers of an art that acted in life.

The Futurists defined themselves *mystics of action* and spoke out in a historical moment when language was being transformed into action: from the declarations of Futurism to the aphasic positions of marginal artists, the role of the word was transformed into broken rhythm or disharmonious music. The more the individual tended to uniqueness, the more he or she exploded and lost the ability to rationally organize reality. Examples were Artaud, Genet, and Strindberg.

The speed of change in the contemporary age was thus higher than the ability of the intellect to conceptualize and understand these changes; the only way to halt them was to enter a dialectic with them without reasoned understanding, but with an artistic sensitivity that it unwittingly comprised.

III.2 *Social Construction of a New Mass Awareness: The Medium of Manifestos*

The analysis of the Futurist Manifestos will be carried out here with a procedure that is perhaps a little unusual: they will be analysed in terms of their similarities with another two types of manifesto. The Manifesto of the Theatre of Cruelty of Antonin Artaud and the Cyborg Manifesto of 1984 written by Donna Haraway regarding the change in position and especially self-awareness of women's situation in relation to new technologies and biopower.

Put this way, it may seem a meaningless interpretative leap, however the analogical connection between these realities is given by the thrust of the will for renewal and socialization of this phenomenon for use by an unwittingly victimized social fascia.

The Futurist Manifestos demanded the need for artistic exchange, unconditional expressive space, not linked to the value of the creative product, but in line with the expressive intention; in fact, they demanded the right to experimentation which the age of industrialization did not value as a cognitive process.

The Manifesto of the Theatre of Cruelty from October 1932, in which Artaud declared the necessity for Western man to enter a culture that knew how to combine the operation of body and mind, and the more recent Cyborg Manifestos of Donna Haraway, are similar declarations of intent for a change in position towards an approach to "virtual" reality lived in a non-virtual manner. The possibility that marginalized social classes could assume power using technology.

In this case too, the liberation from the previous epoch that had created hierarchies of power on sexual bases was surpassed and destroyed by the potential management of power released from membership of gender because of being related to cybernetic systems.

A manifesto introduced into a world of technology in conditions very like those adopted in the Futurist Manifestos to explain and make the transition from a natural sensibility to a machine sensibility. A similar leap being the one from postmodern society to the virtual one.

The analysis of the manifestos has been organized following an order that is not exclusively chronological but also analogical. In other words, I have reconstructed an order of demolition, which to me seemed to clarify some methods that appear to constantly return in the manifestos of Futurism.

I have ideally gathered under the title "Artistic Energy" all the generic manifestos, then all those manifestos that make no direct reference to a particular type of art, but to the very origins of artistic production.

Under the title "The Moving Image" I have included the manifestos relating to the visual arts such as painting and sculpture; in "*La volupté d'être sifflé*" the reference is to the singing and theatrical arts; followed by the "Manifesto of Futurist Woman", to which I have added a fusion between this manifesto, "Marinetti's Multiplied Man and the Religion of the Machine" and the "Cyborg Manifesto" which somehow seem to summarize them within the reality of the new millennium: woman and technology.

In this same vein, we can reread the manifestos of the new art as staking a social claim more than one for art itself. Bourgeois art was waning with the set of values that had made it dominant and the revolution that was prefigured seemed, also in the light of how Futurist ideas were used, a revolution in the observation of the artist, not the means to express art[21]. An observation of changing identity.

III.2.a *Analysis of the Manifestos*

Through the publication of manifestos, Futurism proposed a formal and substantial revision of all the arts and all the customary fields that constitute a country's cultural tradition.

The first manifesto published in 1909 in *Le Figaro* was signed by Marinetti only and proclaimed in a general way the desire to reorganize Italy's social situation through a rebuilding of artistic sensibility.

The tone was categorical and desecrating; the editorial board of the Parisian daily, while publishing its full text, wrote an introduction of diplomatic detachment:

> M. Marinetti, le jeune poète italien et français, au talent remarquable et fougueux, que de retentissantes manifestations ont fait connaître dans tous les pays latins, suivi d'une pléiade d'enthousiastes disciples, vient de fonder l'Ecole du "Futurisme" dont les théories dépassent en hardiesse toutes celles des écoles antérieures ou contemporaines. Le Figaro [...] offre aujourd'hui à ses lecteurs le manifeste des "Futuristes". Est-il besoin de dire que nous laissons au signataire toute la responsabilité de ses idées singulièrement audacieuses et d'une outrance souvent injuste pour des choses eminentement respectables et, heureusement, partout respectées ? Mais il était intéressant de réserver à nous lecteurs la primeur de cette manifestation, quel que soit le jugement qu'on porte sur elle.[22]

The first manifesto basically enclosed the principles that would be found applied with different nuances to the various arts in all subsequent manifestos: a rebellion against the known to make room for the unknown. In particular, they were also applied in substantially the same way: waging a lucid generalized attack on all the more solid and firmly-rooted principles of the art in question.

---

21   P. Martino, *Arte e Rivoluzione*, in G. Lista, *Arte e politica* (Milan: Multhipla, 1980), p. 181.
22   Cf. "Le Figaro", Paris, 20 February 1909.

And often generating a paradox or contradiction in terms: "Art, in fact, can be nothing but violence, cruelty, and injustice", in this way, the path of the impossible was taken to the extreme, to touch the limits of art, language, expression, thus crossing a threshold, and broadening potential.

But what did Marinetti really do? His was never a description or a theory explained point by point, but a path experienced which, in reading it, lets us live the temporality of the story and the experience; like a film with stereo audio and a circular screen that surrounds the spectator, his is a writing without a subject, the subject is the reader who must be able to stop, observe, and move on in reading as in a live dialogue, an interactive writing that requires a reader who is not only active but also circumspect and aware.

The lack of punctuation, probably generated by the habit Marinetti had of dictating to someone else rather than writing in person, stimulates in the reader a need for self-discipline to search for the sense that a reading in one go would not allow.

The first Manifesto of Futurism is difficult to penetrate beyond the shouted declarations of the need for destruction and a declared contempt of the old. Marinetti's medium is not only the publicity ploy of the Manifesto, but also the use of a subjective narrative structure used to communicate an objective position: we find ourselves progressively partaking in a story that was born in a private setting among friends, and then gradually took on the dimensions of a protest against culture, politics, and the dominant tradition. Narration there is, but it is intermittent.

From here came the cultural revolution of the Twentieth Century, from a meeting among friends that ended, as the movement itself would doubtless end, completely off track in a puddle of mud.

The first Manifesto of 20 February 1909 was presented as the result of a narrative introduction which, as in all of Marinetti's stories, would progressively prepare readers and bring them to an emotional involvement in the story. His is a reconstruction of environments, feelings, and memories that come together to form part of the message he intended to communicate and, in the meantime, we have already become immersed in the situation.

> Except that, in place of a sequence that leads to and climaxes in political revolution, Marinetti substitutes the forward march of industrialism. His story is about the trajectory of his own consciousness converging with the path of technological development.
>
> Their point of intersection is made physically explicit in the image of his immersion in the ditch of factory sludge – his body literally embraced by the by-products of industrial progress.

The Manifesto, placed at the story's centre, results in the notion of speed as a plastic value: speed has become a metaphor for temporal progression made explicit and visible. The moving object becomes the vehicle of perceived time, and time becomes a visible dimension of space, once the temporal takes the form of mechanical motion.[23]

The *First Futurist Political Manifesto*, on the occasion of the 1909 General Elections, declared:

We Futurists, whose sole political programme is one of national pride, energy and expansion, denounce before the whole the country the irrevocable shame which a possible clerical victory would bring upon us. [...] We Futurists want a national representation which, freed from mummies, and from every sort of pacifist cowardice, will be ready to extricate us from any snare, and to respond to any outrage whatsoever.

The Futurist poets and writers felt themselves to be those who must act against the "paralysis" of structures. They had no doubts about this, they knew that the function of art is in society, and that therefore through art they should be able to influence the internal structure of even the most rigorous organization.

The Futurists saw industrialism's weak point as its inflexibility, its evolutionary process, but one limited by the use of technique not accompanied by an imaginative quality.

The tone of Futurist proclamations always continued along the line of the first Manifesto; in reality, proclaiming became a way to reaffirm the presence of the movement in all significant events on the political and social planes, as demonstrated by the publications from 1909 of the "Report on the victory of Futurism in Trieste", which reads:

Oh! Anger to feel ourselves, futurist poets, the bearers of explosive ideas, the demolishers of old Italy, imprisoned in a compartment like an eagle in a cage. [...] But our souls hurled into the darkness, ahead of the locomotive that strives to follow us. [...] First, what does Futurism mean? In very simple terms, Futurism means hatred of the past.

And later, in those same years, Marinetti wrote as an introduction to a recital of some Futurist poetry:

---

23   R. Krauss, *Passaggi. Storia della scultura da Rodin alla Land Art* (Milan: Mondadori, 1998).

> In fact, we propose to fight vigorously and destroy the cult of the past. You kill a strong young poet by hurling him against the paper mummy of a great poet who died five hundred years earlier.[24]

The intolerance of roots is evident, of an obligatory membership of family origins, however the conflict was no longer solely of a generational variety; the magnitude of this revolt extended to social potentialities inhibited not by the family of birth, somehow emancipated from the bourgeois revolution through work, but belonged to a deeper and binding social dynamic: cultural affiliation.

The avant-garde revolution was already in some respects identified as the revolt of bourgeois art, constrained to the shackles of academic or economic activities; the fathers in this case were the centres of power to which contemporary art was allied but which, at the same time, it did not abandon.

Moreover, the utopian momentum of a motto such as *"l'art pour l'art"* was understood as the freedom of art to recognize itself only as an expression and not as a value susceptible to judgement by an art market; this was not an overly apt definition for a movement like Futurism which was not indifferent to a possible profit, even though the main motivation was to find a space for expression beyond traditions, but also beyond the market[25].

It should also be borne in mind that such a statement could not exist were it considered within its social destination and, therefore, inserted in a context in which art sought deliverance from both the Church and the authoritarianism of the market.

In some of Marinetti's letters, the consideration fleetingly appears about the non-remuneration of certain evenings where his presence had been requested, such as an evening at Montecatini mentioned by Papini, but which he did not participate in for safety reasons. In that letter of 1913, Marinetti stated that he had earned nothing, but in effect, few letters mention remuneration and perhaps we can say that the economic side was part of the substantial denial of the system into which all avant-garde movements fall.

The "fathers" in this case did not direct but divert new artistic forces, because the world had changed and it was difficult to have examples of life

---

24   F.T. Marinetti, *op. cit.*, p. 245.
25   Cf. Karel Teige, *Il mercato dell'arte* (Turin: Einaudi, 1973).

from the past, they could only be an example of spiritual strength, and of the perfect adaptation of an individual to his or her reality.

What overwhelmed the new man? What was the growing new identity squashed by, because of failing to deal with the past any longer? Futurism perceived the difficulty of its time but did not observe its origins.

It knew that it was necessary to destroy the past and, in this, it carried the flag of innovation against the stale and by-now arid issues of the old-fashioned intellectuals, but did not observe a rule that was as fundamental as it was inconvenient, which means that it did not save that small piece of the past that would allow it to overcome the human banalities that had already transpired. In this it identified with the machines it enthusiastically supported and it reproduced a mechanism of destruction where the attention towards the near future could prevent their own destruction.

In reality, even this type of reflection was superfluous, since the innovative thrust would not have had such a strong pulse had it not been so devastating; hence all that remains is the possibility to investigate what the movement has actually left behind, rather than conjecturing what it might have done.

Marinetti continued:

> Publishers bin the manuscripts of a hungry genius, to spend their money on reprinting masterpieces of distant times. [...] That is why we, in art, politics, and, in short, in every manifestation of life, brutally fight the religion of the past and respect for everything that is ancient. [...] We despise and combat the tyranny of love, which especially among the Latin peoples, scythes the energies of men of action. We combat rancid sentimentality, the obsession with adultery and the conquest of women, in the novel, in the theatre, and in life. In short, we want to replace, in the youthful imagination, the cloying figure of Don Giovanni, the violent domineering ones of Napoleon, Clemenceau and Bleriot. All this, of course, opposes and exasperates the majorities; but we Futurists, we the Far Left of literature, welcome it, since we fear only the easy approval and bland praise of the mediocre.[26]

Again in 1909, the infamous futurist proclamation against sentimentalism was published – *Kill the Moonlight!*

Among the intellectuals, sides were taken pro- or anti-Futurism and in newspapers, curious, not well motivated statements emerged but in which, in the wake of the emotional riots, they felt they must take a stance. Thus, in 1910, in *Le Fanfare della Stampa*, an article on Futurism and the Futurists

---

26 F.T. Marinetti, *op. cit.*, p. 331.

defended by: *Silvio Benco, Elda Gianelli, A. Bellotti, Paolo Arcari, A. Scocchi, V. Cuttin, Augusto Datta, G. Giacomelli, A. Tamanini, etc.*

The polemics against the movement were a part of its life, taking cues and making invaluable observations as it was about the state of the social and intellectual situation it sought to overturn. For example in the Catholic newspaper of Bologna, *"L'Avvenire d'Italia"*, Paul Arcari expressed himself in this way:

> We must speak of Futurism, otherwise we risk through silence to let its ideas insinuate themselves without duly opposing and weakening them. At the same time, public opinion is wrong-footed because the Futurists act with arrogance as long as we talk about them, the strategy of publicity at any cost, as long as they are spoken about.

Without again starting this psychological exegesis, we can observe that Futurism already had a first symptomatic value in its need for immediate echoes. The Futurists were satisfied with a "Decade to accomplish their work". The oldest among them was thirty. "When we are forty, others who are younger and stronger will throw us into the waste basket, like useless manuscripts. – This is what we want to happen!"

The Futurist positions were a pretext to fuel cultural debate and seek to create proselytes for anyone to publish their own opinion, the cultural rambling of ideologies of limited views was nourished by any contribution, be it intellectual, musical, amateur, entrepreneurial, military, technical, artistic, or theatrical; in reality, everything was fodder for the need for transformation and everything was integrated in discussions, comments, and positions.

Andrea Ibels, without worrying himself over age limits, rigidly set out his own theory:

> Every age must have its own artists: and these, once aged, must disappear promptly so that the new aurora can rise. Why should I live tomorrow in the memory of men? It is the radiant sun of today that I wish and want with all the strength of my body and spirit. The Poet no longer wishes to beat time, but to flog and subdue bystanders. This call comes from a French and Italian writer, M., and is the paroxysm of a reaction to two identical and different diseases of the two nations. In France, the cult of social tradition, in Italy the excess of worship of yesterday coming from a lack of contact, which persists, between the writer and society, with the exception of some metropolises.[27]

---

27   Giorgio Kaisserlian, *Vecchia e Nuova Avanguardia,* in "Contributi Martiniani".

III.2.b Art as Energy

The Futurist work of art had its unit of measurement. The emotion evoked by the work was not a measuring unit, nor were the works of the past, but the value was decided absolutely by the rarity of the work, and what can be really rare in a work of art if not the quantity and quality of cerebral energy necessary to produce it[28]?

Therefore, the value of a work of art was measured by the Futurists in terms of its human value; the amount of involvement and dedication; the spontaneity and creative violence that was introduced in its creation: in short, from the necessity of expression which the artist revealed in the momentum.

The nervous energy used in a work of art was the capacity and speed to perceive a different ordering device of the elements. The measurement of such energy was exemplified in terms like those used for a physics formula: "3. In the intellectual sphere, the (non-random) rarity required of a creation is in direct proportion to the amount of energy needed to produce it"[29].

For the current knowledge of physics and mathematics in 1910, space was part of a geometric and non-physical consideration, thus the dimensions of movement, speed, and synthesis were linked to a Cartesian conception that with difficulty satisfied the contemplation of a dimension of movement[30].

In fact, this dimension was more easily expressed through the representation of colour as a space of light that exceeded the space of extension, but had laws connected to the properties of light.

This was the difference between the space of geometric extensions and the moving space of vibrations. A further expansion of space, faster than those of matter and of light, is the space of sound, which was investigated in a rudimentary way by the Futurists through Luigi Russolo's "Art of Noise", or even "The Painting of Sounds, Noises and Smells" by Carlo Carrà in 13 August 1913, in which all the principles of the Futurist renewal were substantially summarized in the fusion of only one single dimension: colours corresponded to smells and sounds, senses were called to an extreme synthesis that was expressed through "plastic, polyphonic and abstract polyrhythmic sets"[31].

---

28   Bruno Corradini, Emilio Settimelli, *Pesi, misure e prezzi del genio artistico*, Milan, 11 March 1914.
29   *Ibid*.
30   P. Francastel, *Il futurismo e il suo tempo* (Paris: Sorbonne, 1965).
31   C. Carrà, *op. cit.* in the text.

This multi-sensory quality was expressed by Carrà in his painting *Il Funerale dell'Anarchico Galli*, and by Boccioni in *La Città che Sale*.

Some years later, the studies by Kandinsky were based on a study of the geometric surface and on the search for a science of art; this need to analyse art from a scientific point of view was directed, even if in this case through other means, to the need for artistic research motivated by a non-utilitarian momentum of knowledge, and by a recognized need for a balance between intuition and calculation in the field of creative forces[32].

This might seem a romantic conception of art, but it was precisely what allowed an extension of the concept of art: valorizing any alogical and irrational creation and confirming its recognition based on what it expressed and not on the basis of what it was; Futurist art demanded the evolutionary quality of creativity, restoring its vital inspiration through experimentation and synthesis.

Key milestones of artistic interpretation, these Futurist principles opened the way to the expressiveness of the Sixties and Seventies, freed creative desire through a "meter" that would decompose works and measure by the amount of energy needed to produce them, and from there declare their value.

This humiliating and doubtful decomposition would afford protection against the cultural snobbery over the artwork which recognized the value of art only if it felt far enough away from concrete life. In this way, Futurism vindicated the possibility for artists to stake their place *within life*.

This empowered them, since in granting them their "incontrovertible" rights of creative freedom, it also imposed some unavoidable duties: the responsibility to be sincere with respect to the discoveries it declared, since it would be this that indicated the use of creative energy in figures, and these figures could then be considered in the assessment of the work in monies. The punishment due to a potential fraud could range from a simple fine to a jail sentence.

This responsibility of knowing how to evaluate one's own creative value would be for the artist a protection and a social stance in every way. While demolition of this mythically constructed character as pure incarnate spirit, would encourage the practicality of the individual to be reunited with creative qualities and know how to integrate them with the social fabric in a functional manner.

---

32   W. Kandinsky, *Punto, Linea, Superficie* (Milan: Adelphi, 1968).

"Art is an exactly measurable cerebral secretion".[33] But the "producer of a creative artistic force must become part of the trade organization that is the muscle of all modern life. Money is one of the most formidably and brutally solid points of the reality in which we live: it will suffice to refer to it in order to eliminate any possibility of errors or unpunished injustices. A good injection of business serum will also introduce directly into the blood of intellectual creators an exact consciousness of their rights and responsibilities".[34]

The measurement of the energy used to create a work used brain functions that had nothing to do with emotions in the sentimental sense but with energies in the pure state, energies that might be used and processed in any desired state.

Art must be the result of a synthesis of energy, the synthesis of a fragment that could bring life to the experimentation of a new multiplicity of signs summarized in turn in new syntheses; the continuous reinvention of fragments dispersed in search of possible new definitions.

This was the idea of the Futurist work of art, which was always accompanied by the rigour of creative honesty, and by sincerity of intent. By means of synthesis, the concepts of space and time would be dominated by speed, and in this way the vital mode of the individual would come ever closer to that of machines.

Speed too was a synthesis: the intuitive synthesis of all the forces in motion, the rapidity of diverting obstacles out of a desire for the new and unexplored. Speed had its own particular connection with the divine, it was *pure* and *absolute*, and reflected the idolatry of the new, what came to human experience as the unknown and the fantastic[35].

"Every Artist can invent a new art, which is the free expression of particular idiosyncrasies of its modernly mad and complicated cerebral constitution [...] i.e. a chaotic, inaesthetic and insolent mix of all the arts that already exist and all those that are and will be created out of an inexhaustible desire for renewal that Futurism will instil in humanity"[36].

Madness was the disruption of the logical relations between things and thus for Futurism was the peak achievement of its purpose, with the Foucauldian awareness that madness was a threshold decided by the sage or the schematized, we know not which.

---

33   Corradini, Settimelli, *op. cit.*
34   *Ibid, Conclusioni.*
35   F.T. Marinetti, *La nuova religione-morale della velocità*, Milan, 11 May 1916.
36   *Ibid.*

III.2.c *The Moving Image*

On 11 April 1910, the *Manifesto of Futurist Painting* (*Technical Manifesto*) came out, signed by Boccioni, Carrà, Russolo, Balla and Severini. In this manifesto emerged the need for a renewal of painting, to integrate new techniques such as Divisionism, in a "congenital complementarism" with any previous pictorial technique deemed necessary for the new expressive sensibility.

> In it, we can read: "…all things move, all things run, all things are rapidly changing. A profile is never motionless before our eyes, but it constantly appears and disappears. On account of the persistency of an image upon the retina, moving objects constantly multiply themselves; their form changes like rapid vibrations, in their mad career. Thus, a running horse has not four legs, but twenty, and their movements are triangular. All is conventional in art. […] What was truth for the painters of yesterday is but a falsehood today." The Manifesto closes with a certainty:
> Our art will probably be accused of tormented and decadent cerebralism. But we shall merely answer that we are, on the contrary, the primitives of a new sensitiveness, multiplied hundredfold…

The Manifestos of Futurism were drawn up personally by exponents of the art they were proclaiming, and it was they themselves who illustrated the theory underlying the painting they put down on canvas.

Boccioni was born in Reggio Calabria to Emilian parents on 19 October 1882; his interests lay between literature and painting and he soon started to collaborate with periodicals in Catania, the city where he studied.

The first known canvases by Boccioni belong to the early years of the Twentieth Century, and the influence of the studies and charisma of the Impressionists on Boccioni's work made itself felt in landscapes and in portraits pervaded by movement, but his true Futurist work had not yet been unfettered.

Little by little, already by 1908, we can observe the first canvases distinguished by a fluidity of strokes, with the line of the movement that confuses the image but defines movement in relation to the surroundings.

Boccioni's images grasp the dialectic movement with the outside which, increasingly rapid and addictive, closes individuals in themselves, almost through the operation of a powerful centripetal force. Movement is expressed with an uncommon fluidity and a shading of contours that helps give the images a character that does not yield as much definition in the detail as it does in the fluidity of the movement: exalting the traits of elasticity and softness which change the very nature of the objects.

In this we can perceive the diversity of the relationship with the surrounding environment: a great flurry which, by generating primal chaos, educates visual perception to a different criterion of the image.

The liveliest and perhaps most curious period of Boccioni's production appears to be the one that began around 1910, thus immediately before the 1911 Manifesto, and it seems that, following the verbalization of the Manifesto, Boccioni's painting unleashed its greater power: *La città che sale, La risata, Visioni simultanee, La strada entra nella casa, Stati d'animo, Gli Addii, Testa + Casa + Luce, Volumi Orizzontali, Fusione di testa e finestra*, until the sculptures: *Sviluppo di una bottiglia nello spazio* by 1912; *Scomposizione di una figura di donna a tavola*, and absolutely indefinable canvases such as *Elasticità* by 1912 or various studies such as *Dinamismo di un corpo umano* by 1913 or also *Dinamismo di un ciclista*.

These are all works just a little later than the Manifesto. The writing of the manifesto seems to have freed more expressive capacity through its approach to a pictorial language steeped in experiments and mixtures of reality, such as that of the individual with the surrounding environment.

In this case, the writing nourished by defining the exploratory fields of art.

In 1914, Boccioni published for editions of *Poesia*, the first official organ of Futurism, a dossier entitled *Pittura e Scultura Futuriste, Dinamismo Plastico* in which, in addition to indicating the intentions and style of Futurist art, he clearly explained the continuity and diversity between Impressionism and Futurism.

In their search for a dialectic between the inside and the outside in a world that was changing before their eyes, the Impressionists had analysed reality to be able to observe it in more detail and to associate shapes and colours in such a way that reality was transmitted just as it impressed their optic fibres. For this same reason, the Impressionists seemed to suffer from the impact of the new external reality in motion with the breaking up of forms, and for this reason their work was incomplete.

The new dimension that had been discovered by the Impressionists was rendered by a lack of depth; the visual strength of the colours brought forth the image, smoothed the planes, and let the new likeness take shape: the environment and its relationship with objects changed; for the first time, the limelight was not of the subject but of the influence that the surrounding atmosphere created on the subject, the outside made its encroachment felt on the inside, the individual, and the object.

The lack of depth, and the importance of the atmosphere changed the priorities of impression of the subjects on the canvas. Hence the importance of colour and light; in the eyes of the Impressionists, the world was a nucleus of vibrations, as it probably was to the eyes of Van Gogh. Vibrations that were rendered as colour: the object as a centre of vibrations, and for the Futurists, these vibrations took a form and became directions, lines, and objects that sometimes blended in indefinable vortices, at other times showed a more typical determination of design lines.

Many of Fortunato Depero's creations were models for advertising campaigns, such as the famous one for Campari, while sketches by Boccioni were often used to represent movement on propaganda posters, such as *The Fist*.

This is what they meant by the plastic mood:

> It is through this new concept of motion of matter, expression as accidental values, interpretation and sentimental fiction of the truth, but as a plastic equivalent of life itself, that we come to the dynamic definition of the impression, which is the intuition of life. ...this is one of the bases of Futurist Painting.[37]

The synthetic quality of Futurist art lay precisely in this unique way of perceiving the outside world, while Impressionist art and its evolution in fragmented Cubism, decomposing the object and in this way depriving it of its inner life and killing the emotion, were scientific procedures necessary for renewal, but that must be transcended to bring a new unity to the object, enriched by its fresh composition of colours, sensations, vibrations, but in an alive uniqueness and in its movement.

> There is a barbaric element in modern society in which we find inspiration. Therefore, we do not want to redo the movement of the crowds and the episodes that pass under our nose. We want to search for the necessities of life in the unconscious, as they arise, the laws for a new – completely new! – plastic consciousness.[38]

Three elements were essential in Futurist painting: dynamism, modern life, and formal and chromatic complementarism.

Emotion was the measure of dynamism, it halted the deconstructive tendency of analysis and legitimated arbitrariness. Cubism was dictated

---

37   G. Balla, *Manifesto dei pittori futuristi*, Florence 1912.
38   F.T. Marinetti, *op. cit.*, p. 74.

by reason, Futurism by feeling. Reason tended to build a permanent static vision of reality, sensation left it the gift of movement and intuition, one was the concrete backbone of the real, the other its variable infinite, and mobile action.

The liberation of Futurist art was probably nourished by the verbalization it enjoyed through the writing of its Manifestos; the word staked a claim on creation, the integral energy of the group belonging to a kindred micro-reality meant that this reality could become contagious.

Studies on the action of active minorities carried out in this regard in psychology are surely explanatory of similar dynamics. What is certain is that this becomes possible when the social cleavage is already ongoing beneath the surface.

After Boccioni's death in 1916, the master of futurist painters became Giacomo Balla, the eldest of the group:

> Balla was of small stature, almost round, and rosy-faced, with a stiff pointed beard. From his blue eyes, flickered pins of pungent irony. He looked, investigated, dreamed, scanned and discovered, always. He would stand for hours on a street corner to grasp and analyse the most curious vibrations, the most difficult and unthinkable chromatic problems of reality. [...] He divided the colour of a jet of water and a ray of the sun. He fixed on canvas the luminous mathematical and geometric divisionism of the vibrating prism of a great arc lamp. A painter-scientist, he painted authentic eigenstates of mood and psychic fluids of invisible realities.[39]

The *Futurist Reconstruction of the Universe* was written by Balla and Depero and came out in 1915. In it, in addition to details of the new universe, indications were given of new living beings suitable to inhabit it: the Futurist toy, the artificial landscape, the metallic animal (a fusion of art + science). But this second part of Futurism would be condemned for the various similarities it presented with certain productions of art and concurrent virtual theories.

In his *Dinamismo Plastico* Umberto Boccioni said:

> In the mood, plastic feeling is the material clothing of the spirit. And with this, eventually the creating artist does not watch, observe, measure nor weigh; he feels, and the sensations that envelope him dictate the shapes and colours that arouse the emotions that made him act plastically. Should we abandon painting? [...] I do not know. Unfortunately, the human mind operates between two equally endless horizon lines: the absolute and the relative, and between

---

39   MART, Historical Archive, Fondo Depero, ms. 3822.

these our work marks the broken and painful line of possibility. Never fear our young friends therefore: there will never be enough audacity to leave the strict law of art that each exerts.[40]

In 1912, with the publication of the volume *Futurist Painting and Sculpture*, after exalting the power of Italian genius, Boccioni advocated and predicted a flattening of all the Nordic and especially Teutonic artistic trends, thanks to Italian Futurist Art.

With Boccioni's Plastic Dynamism, Futurism attempted a balance between the parts:
  – Synthesis of form and colour
  – Lines-force
  – Solidification of Impressionism
  – Dynamic Complementarism
  – Interpenetration of planes.

The *Manifesto dei Pittori Futuristi* 11 February 1910.

"Only that art which finds its own elements in the environment that surrounds it is vital," the rebellion of the Futurist painters was associated with that of the poets, identifying in machines the true social subject that would transform the future.

Singing, and the exaltation of transatlantic liners, aeroplanes, trains, roaring engines, were associated with the appearance of new social figures excluded from progress, that therefore substantiated limits and possible effects.

These criteria had already appeared in Balla's *Polittico dei viventi*: *Il Mendicante* (1902), *I Malati* (1903), *La pazza* (1905), *Il contadino* (1907).

Tradition for Futurism was a voluntary cerebral laziness. Again, in the conclusions of the Manifesto we can read at point 6: "Rebel against the tyranny of words: 'Harmony' and 'Good Taste' and other loose expressions that can be used to destroy the works of Rembrandt, Goya, Rodin."

In the Manifesto of Futurist Painters of 1910, the year in which Marinetti met Boccioni and other artists involved in the movement, the organizational chart of the movement was presented in this way printed entirely on the back, to then reappear on each subsequent manifesto:

THE DIRECTORATE OF THE FUTURIST POETRY MOVEMENT
F.T. Marinetti – Paolo Buzzi – A. Palazzeschi – E. Cavacchioli – Corrado Govoni – Libero Altomare – Luciano Folgore – G. Carrieri – G. Manzella-

---

40   U. Boccioni, *Grande Esposizione. Boccioni Pittore e Scultore Futurista*, (Florence: SPES, 1916).

Frontini – Mario Bétuda – Aura D'alba – Armando Mazza – Dinamo Correnti – Francesco Cangiullo, etc.
PAINTING
U. Boccioni – C.D. Carrà – L. Russolo – Giacomo Balla
G. Severini – Ardengo Soffici, etc.
MUSIC
Balilla Pratella
SCULPTURE
Umberto Boccioni
FEMALE ACTION
The poetess, Valentine de Saint-Point
ART OF NOISE
Luigi Russolo.
The Directorate of the Futurist Movement: Corso Venezia, 61 – Milan.

In 1912, several important Manifestos were presented for the reconstruction of the sensitivity desired by Futurism: The *Prefazione al Catalogo delle Esposizioni di Parigi, Londra, Berlino, Bruxelles, Monaco, Amburgo, Vienna, etc.* by Boccioni, Carrà, Russolo, Balla, Severini of February 1912.

The repetitive and redundant declaration of Futurist art in each manifesto, which also returned in this foreword was the centrality of the spectator. Even in painting the object was no longer the subject.

To intensify aesthetic emotion, they painted bundles of lines that corresponded to the forces in play on the canvas: for a brawl or for the details of a crowd, sets of lines were used that involve observers in a feeling like a visual fight to understand the image, making them feel like sharers in the action described.

"Not painting sounds, but their vibrant intervals. Not painting diseases, but their symptoms and consequences"[41]. Painting moods, as Boccioni already did; in effect, what Futurist art did in every work was to seize the transformation, that which in an object, in a subject, in a situation, was not yet defined: what was in power, pure movement. In this lay "Futurism", the search for what would become visible, and not in representing or showing what already existed.

Objects multiplied in the movement, hence the classic affirmation of Futurism that "...a running horse has not four legs, but twenty...". The paintings aimed at creating an emotional environment, but to create communication they were in some way forced to provide material indications of the spiritual world they referred to.

---

41   U. Boccioni, ibid.

These references built a bridge – they say in their Manifesto – without which what would remain of their work would only be the destruction of the reality that in fact they implemented in every expression.

In conclusion, they dictated three new conceptions of painting, fundamental to enter the Futurist language:

1) The resolution of the volumes in a picture that respect the proportions of the objects.

2) The objects reproduced as lines-forces that let them achieve the brand-new Futurist plastic dynamism.

3) The creation of the picture's emotional environment, "a synthesis of the various abstract rhythms of each object".

"Art [was] creation through images of thought"[42] according to the group of young Russians who gathered around the year 1915 to form the "Moscow Linguistic Circle". Scientific studies of language originated their thesis on the assumption that poetry is a precise way of thinking, a peculiarity of thought that organizes the unknown into sequences of known images.

But the art of language, like the art of images, in addition to a capacity of original reorganization, was also the fruit of a specific condition joined to a core of human experience that was equally unpredictable in its reactions and, in Futurist art, the only real constant was continuous change and the search for a plastic assimilation of this change.

In the rather terroristic conjectures of G. Debord, the father of Situationist International, in *La Société du Spectacle*, there is a different use of the concept of image, in this case referring to spectacle. For Debord, spectacle was not a collection of images, but a social relationship between people, mediated by images, but as soon as art was an art of change it became a pure expression of impossible change: the art of the avant-garde. And the greater the change it demanded, the more effective the implementation of it surpassed it[43].

The characteristic of Futurism was, in all its expressive forms, the image of movement: the interpenetration of form and time in a structure that was sometimes narrative, sometimes pictorial, sometimes musical, theatrical or sculptural. But in all its expressions, the power of involvement and the main communication would always be entrusted to the often-spectacular potentiality of a transformation that was simultaneous with the work.

---

42   Cf. Viktor Sklovskij, *L'arte come procedimento*, in "I Formalisti Russi" ed. T. Todorov (Turin: Einaudi, 1968).

43   G. Debord, *op. cit.*, p. 83.

Observers were sharers in the movement of Futurist Art because they were in turn involved and integrated through the transfer of sensations. The quality of the Futurist change seemed then to be entrusted almost exclusively to its temporal path.

On 11 April 1912, the *Manifesto of Futurist Sculpture* came out, written by Umberto Boccioni.

Its central idea revealed sculpture to be the art that was most lagging behind in the evolution of form, since it represented the direct contact of people with matter, and as long as the essence of this relationship had not been renewed, the references would inevitably always return to rebuild sculptures with Greek or Egyptian elements.

Boccioni developed the idea of the "interpenetration of planes". For him sculpture aimed to rebuild the abstraction of planes and volumes that determine forms.

In fact, he was to be the only Futurist sculptor who would delve into this work on the subject, his studies on the human body and the work *Development of a Bottle in Space* from 1912 were the result of reflection on the duplicity of the relationship of the object (and subject) with its outside, the environment, and its interior, its defined form.

In this reflection, we can rediscover the expression of a difficulty in relation to the subject that arose in an environment that for him was invasive and required continuous interaction, like the new urban situation of the early years of the century, and an interiority which, entering into a relationship with the requests of the exterior, threatened to become devastated and emptied.

Boccioni seems to have grasped both difficulties in the creation of matter, trying to find a double movement between the outside and inside of the object, two types of movement that enter a relationship and produce a work which also seems in motion, but is actually open on two fronts: unfinished inside, hence as an object, and unfinished outside since it is "mobile".

This is the sculpture of the environment yearned for by Boccioni in his manifesto, through which he would develop Plastic Dynamism, that "ideal bridge which joins the exterior plastic infinite to the interior plastic infinite"[44].

From these expressions, it may seem a purely abstract, indecisive concept, perhaps, suffice to observe the work to understand what Boccioni

---

44   Vv Aa, *Da Boccioni a Sironi. Il mondo di Margherita Sarfatti* (Milan: Skira, 1997), p. 210.

wanted to create in reality: we see nothing but movement, both the interior one for the transformation of the individual in relation to the change of the environment, and the outward movement necessary for survival in the new fast universe of the machine.

Boccioni's firm decisive stroke in the figure seems part of his own secure physical figure with attitude.

The Pre-Futurist Boccioni was still regular in his forms, albeit full of dramatic energy. Slowly, even with the contact with French Cubism, the figures became even more dynamic and exploded in confused and fused images of objects, subjects, landscapes, and environments, so that his painting was criticized by Margherita Sarfatti as being so busy chasing the momentary that it missed out on the infinite[45].

The Futurist intention was perhaps neither one nor the other, conceivably it was only the victim of the involvement that distinguished it in every manifestation.

On 27 April 1910, Marinetti's "Futurist Speech to the Venetians" appeared:

> When we cried out: 'Let's Kill the Moonlight!' we thought of you, old Venice soaked in romance! But now our voice is amplified, and we will add in high notes 'Free the world from the tyranny of love! We are stuffed with erotic adventures, luxury, sentimentalizing, and nostalgia"! Oh! How we shall dance, on that day! Oh! How we shall applaud the lagoons, to induce them to destruction! [...] We will all be madly cheerful, we, the last rebel students of this too-wise world![46]

Again in 1910, he delivered a speech against academies and erudite scholars, *Contro i Professori*: "We are opposed to this superhuman Greek, born from the dust of libraries, Man multiplied by his own work, the enemy of the book, the friend of personal experience, the pupil of the Machine, avid cultivator of his own will, polished in the flash of his inspiration, equipped with feline flair, rapid calculations, instinctively wild, intuition, cunning, temerity. Now, courage is precisely the raw material"[47].

And the *Futurist Speech to the English* (proclaimed at London's Lyceum Club):

45   *Ibid.*, p. 210.
46   F.T. Marinetti, *op. cit.*, p. 190.
47   *Ibid.*, p. 306.

To a certain degree you are the victims of your traditionalism and its medieval trappings, in which there persists a whiff of archives and a rattling of chains that hinder your precise and carefree forward march. [...] Most of all I reproach you for your maddening cult of aristocracy. No one admits to being a *bourgeois* in England: everyone despises his neighbour and calls him a *bourgeois*. You have an obsessive mania for being always *chic*. For the love of being *chic* you renounce passionate action, violence of heart, exclamations, shouts, and even tears.[48]

Futurism enhanced individuals' ability to redeem themselves from social links, freeing creativity and expression over social belonging: in this it is difficult to fully believe in the Futurist revolution as a revolution of bourgeois art.

In part, it was because its approaches ranked it more with a capacity for redemption through the action of its own bourgeois flair, while on the other hand, it used this available subversive force for all situations of imbalance between expression and society, therefore hoping to overcome the social hierarchies, crossing them and dwelling in them transversely.

Futurism affirmed the most subversive values of its era, and the artists who were part of it were witnesses of the demise of art that involved them. Marinetti's free enthusiasm seems to have gradually taken on the appearance of a last humanitarian impulse of an ancient heritage, much more than he himself was aware of.

Carlo Carrà, writing to Gino Severini on 3 June 1914, therefore with Futurism in full flow, expressed himself with these words:

The action of Marinetti will increasingly adopt this social character. Whatever you want to make us, because of the tireless and little reflective activity of Marinetti and Boccioni, Futurism will head increasingly towards a character which I believe deeply traditionalist and humanitarian.[49]

The words of Carrà were dictated by a temperament that made him completely the opposite of both Boccioni and Marinetti. The frenetic activity of the pair opposed the patience and ability to restore every experience to a basic continuity.

In this case, the most sensitive personalities were most affected by external events and were not freed if not in frenzied activity.

---

48   F.T. Marinetti, *op. cit.*, p. 281.
49   Giuseppe Raimondi, *Gli archivi del Futurismo*, in "*Comunità*" (Milan: October 1959), pp. 62-69.

La volupté d'être sifflé.

On 11 January 1911, Balilla Pratella wrote the *Manifesto of Futurist Musicians*, followed by *Futurist Music*, and *The Technical Manifesto*.

The Futurists' strategy was to strengthen their identity as different artists through the mutual publication of a manifesto of open protest against the status quo, then proceed to give theoretical directives on how they conceived their art, and how the approach to give life to a new version of that same art must be technically conceived.

The next step in the Futurist's cultural destruction was the *Manifesto of Futurist Musicians* written by Francesco Balilla Pratella:

> 4. To keep at a distance from commercial or academic circles, despising them, and preferring a modest life to bountiful earnings acquired by the selling of art. [...] 7. To proclaim that the reign of the singer must end, and that the importance of the singer in relation to a work of art is the equivalent of the importance of an instrument in the orchestra.

Which found its natural continuation and fulfilment on 29 March 1911 with the *Technical Manifesto of Futurist Music*, this too written by Balilla Pratella. The manifesto begins in this way:

> All innovators were logically futurists, in relation to their own times. Palestrina would judge Bach crazy, just as Bach would have judged Beethoven, and Beethoven would have judged Wagner. Rossini boasted of having finally understood Wagner's music by reading it upside down! Verdi, after a hearing the Tannhäuser Overture, called Wagner mad in a letter to his friend.[50]

The Futurist Musicians, in the name of F. Balilla Pratella who signed the manifesto, intended music as the result of the synthesis of harmony, in the various possible combinations and from the multiple relationships ensuing from it would flourish the Futurist melody, which relies on an *enharmonic* mode.

Of crucial importance would be the musicians, their acoustic sensibility and performance skills, the experience that had refined their art; instrumental technique would evolve through experimentation; every accent of passion and knowledge would enrich the expressiveness of the melody.

The forms declared wholly adherent to Futurist freedom were: the symphonic poem, both orchestral and vocal, and Opera.

---

50   Francesco Balilla Pratella, *La musica futurista*, in "Manifesto tecnico", 29 March 1911.

In *La distruzione della Quadratura* written by F. Balilla Pratella and published on 18 July 1912, the rhythm is analysed and decomposed geometrically.

Futurist music too was characterized by an absolute freedom of rhythm, the main rhythmic unit being represented by movement, while the bourgeois framework, orderly and predictable in its composition, was replaced by the intuition of instinctive rhythmic solutions. The Manifesto concludes with a eulogy of disorder: "an OLD POLICEMAN whose legs are not good enough to run with; WE FUTURISTS ARE CREATING THE NEW ORDER OF DISORDER."

The Manifesto of Playwrights.
"*Entre toutes les formes littéraires, celle qui a une portée futuriste plus puissante est certainement l'œuvre théâtrale.*"

The *Manifesto of Futurist Playwrights* came out on 11 January 1911, and was signed by F. T. Marinetti. Because theatre can change, and can in turn be a tool to communicate the new, immediate success was despised, which would be the result of a work understandable by already consolidated culture, thus not expressing the new.

The mediocrity of known schemes made every success suspect; being understood by the prevailing sensibility meant not being able to tarnish it, in other words would mean having been absorbed by its lazy and distracted opulence, which was a translation of "failure" in Futurist words.

Futurist theatre was in practice a spectacle constituted mostly in the theatre of variety. The technique, dialogues, and psychological pedantries made classical theatre verbose and didactic. The new Futurist synthesis arose from the dynamism that in theatre resolves in improvisation: the uncalculated experimental act and the combination of speed and anti-traditionalism.

The attraction for a hectic, complex, cynical and elusive life, merged in synthetic theatre with a cerebral conception of art in which only what was still a source of life and newness applied and survived, nothing was susceptible to exclusion if it smelt of lived experience, if the energies used to create it were aimed at overcoming cultural deformations.

"We are finally teaching authors and actors the voluptuousness of being whistled at"[51].

---

51   Filippo Tommaso Marinetti, *Manifesto dei Drammaturghi Futuristi*, 11 January 1911.

The *Manifesto of Futurist Synthetic Theatre* is dated 11 January 1915 and signed by F.T. Marinetti, Emilio Settimelli and Bruno Corradini.

Having overcome the formalities of the manifestos, Futurist theatre presented itself most successfully in a laboratory of experiments on the transformation of the human figure and thus of its presentation.

Also in this situation, the objective was to decrease the distance between man and object, with the intention of dehumanizing man and humanizing the object.

Some examples are: the independent theatre of Anton Giulio Bragaglia (1923-1936), which although never swearing allegiance to the movement was perhaps the most daring theatrical interpreter; the fantastic mechanical constructions of Fortunato Depero; the attempts at irrational theatre of Gino Gori; the theatre of colour of Achille Ricciardi. The synthetic theatre echoed many of the experiments of French or German theatre, but interpreted the most extreme tendencies in the Italian sense.

> Craignez tout du Passé vermoulu. Espérez tout de l'Avenir. Ayez confiance dans le Progrès qui a toujours raison, même quand il a tort, parce qu'il est le mouvement, la vie, la lutte, l'espoir. Gardez-vous bien d'intenter des procès au Progrès. Qu'il soit imposteur, perfide, assassin, voleur, incendiaire, le Progrès a toujours raison.[52]

Progress is always right, said Marinetti, also because, once implemented, its process is almost always unstoppable.

III.2.d *Manifesto of the Futurist Woman*

The *Manifesto of the Futurist Woman* was drawn up by Valentine de Saint-Point in Paris and is dated 25 March 1912.

Little is known about the poetess author of the manifesto; she was a Parisian friend of Marinetti who seems to have accepted the challenge almost as a provocation; she subscribed to Papini's journal probably because Marinetti had recruited and convinced her to.

In a letter to Giovanni Papini, undated but certainly sent in 1914, Marinetti asked Papini to publish the new Manifesto of Futurism in *Lacerba* which continued the movement's artistic action, using it and transforming it into political action.

At the bottom of the page of this same letter Marinetti sent the address of the poetess Valentine de Saint-Point together with numerous other

---

52   Filippo Tommaso Marinetti, *Le Futurisme* (Paris: Ed. Sansot et C.ie, 1911), p. 117.

addresses of intellectuals and non: *Madame de Saint-Point, 19, Avenue de Tourville Paris, Another Subscriber.*

For a period, de Saint-Point was a supporter of the magazine *Lacerba*. Later, we find her as a dancer of "ideist" dance in which she showed herself to the audience fully covered, including her face, so as to speak only through her body.

With its geometric figures, essential motion and freedom from sentimental smoothness, the dance of de Saint-Point resulted in the eyes of Marinetti still too "psychologizing" thanks to its excessive sophistication, and in the *Manifesto of Futurist Dance* of 1917 he wrote:

> Valentine de Saint-Point conceived an abstract metaphysical dance that was supposed to translate pure thought without sentimentality and without sexual ardour. Her *Métachorie* consisted of mimed poems and dance.[53]

But the feminine danced for Marinetti could not be the expression of a series of geometric and cerebral poses, the sensitivity should transpire from the body, from the eyes and gestures and especially "Why wearing a Merovingian helmet and cover the eyes?"[54].

The *Manifesto of the Futurist Woman* bears as an aside some verses of the first Manifesto of Futurism:

> We will glorify war – the world's only hygiene – militarism, patriotism, the destructive gesture of freedom-bringers, beautiful ideas worth dying for, and scorn for woman.

And then it begins:

> "Humanity is mediocre. The majority of women are neither superior nor inferior to the majority of men. They are all equal. They all merit the same scorn," and again: "It is absurd to divide humanity into men and women. It is composed only of femininity and masculinity."

The criticism in this case turned against feminism, considered the fruit of cleverness. Also in this case the forces evoked were violence, cruelty, "sublime injustice", the division of humanity into categories of strong and weak, categories borrowed from the laws of nature; the brutalization of life is equivalent to re-appropriating the quality and creative freedom that mankind has stifled under the veil of social order.

---

53   *Ibid.*, 147.
54   *Ibid.*

Le mépris de la femme.

This opens an interesting chapter of Futurist production; Marinetti dedicated a good part of his book *Le Futurisme* to the question of women.

Women were publicly despised; although specified with extreme accuracy, the meaning of this statement is still misinterpreted. The contempt referred to the concept of woman in vogue at that time, the role and expectations covered by the role of women in the early years of the Twentieth Century.

An indolent woman, ailing in her physique and intellect, made marginal by male domination, was seen as treacherous and destructive, useless socially but perhaps even privately.

The female figure was still in search of its own positive and socially recognized identity, a woman with a power equal to man and free to choose her own destiny in line with her intimate propensity was yet to come: Futurism as an exaltation of force, which would appear much more like an exhortation to an inner force of reaction, extended in this case also to the situation of women.

Marinetti's ideal urged the possibility of a woman free from her own genetic slavery as a procreator, to achieve a female identity free to choose serenely between her creative potential in a biological sense and the care of her creative potential in an intellectual sense.

In a lucid criticism of traditional society, Marinetti also assimilated female education to a few limiting rudiments devoid of useful tools for the healthy development of creativity and the formation of a self-reliant individual:

> Quant à la prétendue infériorité de la femme, nous pensons que si le corps et l'esprit de la femme avaient subi, à travers une longue série de générations, une éducation identique à celle reçue par l'esprit et le corps de l'homme, nous pensons, dis-je, qu'il serait possible de parler raisonnablement d'égalité entre les deux sexes. Il est certain, néanmoins, que dans son état actuel d'esclavage intellectuel et érotique, la femme, se trouvant dans une condition d'infériorité absolue au point de vue du caractère et de l'intelligence, ne peut guère être qu'un instrument législatif médiocre. C'est pourquoi nous défendons avec la plus grande ferveur le droit des suffragettes, tout en plaignant leur enthousiasme enfantin pour le misérable et ridicule droit de voter. Car nous sommes convaincus qu'elles s'en empareront avec ferveur, et nous aideront ainsi, involontairement, à détruire cette grande balourdise, faite de corruption et de banalité qu'est devenue aujourd'hui le Parlementarisme.[55]

---

55   Cfr. Filippo Tommaso Marinetti, *Le mépris de la femme*, in "Le Futurisme",
      (Paris: Ed. Sansot et C.ie, 1911), pp. 60-61.

In the *Manifesto of Futurist Woman*, Valentine de Saint-Point mustered women's cruelty, that quality cleaved from sentimentality which resulted in an action strictly linked to primary needs. The freedom and dignity of the individual were therefore related to the rigour with which the most urgent needs were pursued. In this sense, the individual-automaton was foreshadowed: unable to bond and feel compassion, which would leave even Artaud in the most painful solitude.

Cruelty was the main theme, the obsessive idea, and at the same time the sense of knowledge that Artaud used in theorizing a theatre of cruelty: a scenario as real as life that was not masked in front of a life that was essentially cruel.

Lucidity in suffering that led past the threshold of collective understanding, widespread perception, of the reality to come.

The *theatre of cruelty* was the scenario of the vital life, devoid of social platitudes, a vital level perceived as truer to those who already lived it for its own natural or socially induced quality: those who had no protection from any kind of social category; who, being on the margins, availed themselves painfully of the danger of isolation.

In the case of Artaud, however, there was no conscious choice, there was only a violent need to travel the road even if it led to a point of no return. A life without aims and horizons was spiritually perceived as a non-life, a life purely biological but incomplete.

"WOMEN, FOR TOO LONG TORN BETWEEN MORALS AND PREJUDICES, RETURN TO YOUR SUBLIME INSTINCT: TO VIOLENCE AND CRUELTY".

It is also true that Futurism was unable to indicate routes of subversion other than the path of violence.

In fact, many criticisms of contemporary art have glimpsed bourgeois art in it, the cultural revolution through which the bourgeoisie tried to curb the rise of the Socialist revolution.

Culture and art were seeking a closer relationship with the practical life, avant-garde art placed itself on a working plane, intervened politically, transformed its artistic action into political action with extreme simplicity, extended the fields of revolution not only to traditionally "cultural" areas in the high sense, but dealt with cuisine, with sound as a noise in the vein of the noise of the city; dealt more with the quality of creative energies than the quality of the work, dismantled the bourgeois cliché of art and literature "to be seen" and tried to reconcile aesthetic creativity with technical production; attempting to break through the barriers of daily life, entering creative impetus alongside practical quality[56].

However, there remained Benn's doubtful reflection in consideration of the artist's social role: "Can artistic greatness ever be historically effective, can it be inserted in the process of becoming?"[57]. For Benn, the artists' possibilities were substantially limited within phenomenological models of the soul: they found it difficult to leave the interior to become part of history.

"The bourgeois," Soffici wrote in a fairly late text, "is no longer a man of order and a slowcoach: he is avant-garde, revolutionary, and extremist."

In all of this for the bourgeois artist the value of work changed, work as an artistic activity could either join the production system and thus become an artistic object reproduced in series, losing its aura of irreproducible uniqueness; or could subvert the value of work and restore value to creation, denying any production value:

> In different terms, the avant-garde is the place where, having denied all values, human work tries to regain its own specificity or difference, to satisfy authentic needs and desire, to express the immediacy of its 'natural being' taking artistic experience as a model, which is in itself the exemption from work and a demand for love.[58]

The Cyborg Manifesto

> A cyborg is a cybernetic organism, a hybrid of machine and organism, a creature of social reality as well as a creature of fiction. Social reality is lived social relations, our most important political construction, a world-changing fiction.

A series of considerations can be done looking at potential "contemporary" rebound of futurism which link the Futurist discourse of the individual in relation to the machine. In this case, for example, the Cyborg Manifesto represents the hybridization of feelings on one hand and the transformation of the body on the other, synthesized in the woman as a subject in transformation towards a different social identity.

It can be useful at this point to read Marinetti's discourse on *Multiplied Man and the Reign of the Machine*. The elimination of the harmful

---

56   Cfr. U. Artioli (ed.), *Il viandante e la sua orma* (Bologna: Cappelli, 1981).
57   Gottfried Benn, *op. cit.*, p. 33.
58   Pietro Bonfiglioli, *Dopo l'avanguardia. L'avventura estetica della critica senza sicurezza*, p. 43, in U. Artioli, *op. cit.*

influence that the romantic veil might have on the individual could only occur through the search for a new balance between man and the machine. Love with a capital "L" -as Marinetti called it- the way of the ancients represented a danger for the new world: it distracted, slowed and obscured the lucidity of intuition. With this conviction, Marinetti proceeded in his dissertation in triumph for the machine, his new object of love.

A relationship that saw the interaction between different elements belonging to different natures and that, precisely for this reason, changed one another.

The sentimental individual must necessarily reduce his or her emotional charge in managing a technical tool, the accuracy of the technical left no possibility for the deviant potential of sentiments.

In Futurism, sentimentality thus assumed the connotation of a pathology of the spirit that failed to rediscover its innate cruelty and lucidity in the narrow schemes of past idolatry. To all of which, Marinetti opposed the idolatry of the future, of the machine, of the lucid spirit.

> [...] we aspire to a non-human type in which will be abolished moral pain, goodness, affection and love, only corrosive poisons of the inexhaustible vital energy, only switches of our mighty physiological electricity. [...] To prepare the formation of this non-human type and mechanical man multiplied by externalization of his will, it is individually necessary to decrease the need for affection, not yet destructible, that man carries in his veins. (F. T. Marinetti)

And again:

> They will be equipped with unexpected organs: bodies adapted to the needs of an environment made of continuous shocks. We can now perceive a development in the form of a prow from the external projection of the sternum, which will be even more significant because the future man will become an ever-better aviator. (F. T. Marinetti)

Marinetti's man was not yet born, but was in incubation; we can already see the features of the poet's intuition, and in 1998 we could calmly read the words of Haraway and embody in some of her weary multi-justified explanations a clear awareness of an intellectual paternity that might seem reckless, but, in reality, was only pure analogy, in this case too.

> Liberation rests on the construction of the consciousness, the imaginative apprehension, of oppression, and so of possibility. The cyborg is a matter of fiction and lived experience that changes what counts as women's experience in the late twentieth century. This is a struggle over life and death, but the

boundary between science fiction and social reality is an optical illusion. [...]
By the late twentieth century, our time, a mythic time, we are all chimeras,
theorized and fabricated hybrids of machine and organism; in short, we are
cyborgs. The cyborg is our ontology, it gives us our politics. The cyborg is
a condensed image of both imagination and material reality, the two joined
centres structuring any possibility of historical transformation.[59]

We are all chimeras and hybrids, says Haraway, the fusion of two
realities, the material and immaterial that were the first theorizers in the
Futurists, through cybernetics the contemporary has fed the concrete
possibility to live the virtual.

The Cyborg Manifesto seems both the concretization of Futurism's
fantasies, and a continuation of the imaginative capacity to create parallel
realities, external both for the body and for society, but which are self-
generated by instruments to boost the mind, the cerebral energy that Balla,
Marinetti, Depero, Fillia, Prampolini, and Russolo spoke of: "To prepare
the formation of this non-human type and mechanical man multiplied by
externalization of his will, it is individually necessary to decrease the need
for affection, not yet destructible, that man carries in his veins"[60].

This excerpt taken from *Multiplied Man and the Reign of the Machine*
joins the thought of the futurists to that of the Cyborg reality, a conjunction
between past and present without signs of time which endorsed the idea
that the condition of estrangement of the artist in revolt combined well with
other social figures in revolt and transformation who, through the label of
belonging to an enigmatic world of the future, circumvent the present.

The dimension of Futurism in its social context was one of tangency, as
were these Cyborg Manifestos, backwashes of activated reality that were
originally retrieved by means of art, these latter, contemporary ones, by
means of technologies.

In the industrialized, postmodern world, seemingly individuals could
only find a direction if they granted the body interpenetration with a
machine, in this case with technology.

In both cases, and in both epochs, it was the subject who, having lost
interest in the outside world, could only generate art from his or her own
interiority. Art had lost the function of a "blurry margin of the human soul",
its dominion had become central in modern culture, just as the subjectivity
of the individual was central.

---

59   Donna Haraway, *Simians, Cyborgs, and Women. The Reinvention of Nature*,
      (London: Free Associations Book, 1991), p. 19.
60   F.T. Marinetti, *L'uomo moltiplicato e il Regno della macchina*, *op. cit.*, p. 300.

In the case of the Cyborg Manifesto, as in the Manifestos of Futurism, we are faced with an explanation of the change in sensibility. Haraway immerses the reader in the "post-gender" cybernetic world: she explains the historicized Western world's nodal points of liberation and passing which still seems to depend ideologically and politically on the myth of original unity and casts a prismatic look at the reality of the cyborg which instead has no memory since it is without history. Here too is a new context of the interruption of narration. From here begins the gripping description of the new relationship and the new sensibility and motivation of the cyborg as an independent element, infinitely free, an inhabitant of space, seeking links not of an identity type but of affinity.

Its identity is floating; therefore, it cannot be based on itself for contact with the outside: the link between subjects changes the reference and relies upon the new relational network generated by the unity of intent, or even by the sharing of one and the same political front. The identity is fluctuating because it can only be entrusted to the subject.

It seems to me that the term "political" in this context is used more in a relational sense than in the traditional meaning of the supporting party or ideology. The political front that supports the cyborg is a freedom of action without aprioristic or atavistic limitations, which have joined an ethic of common action, aware of the transformation of social boundaries that have been literally translated by revisiting the total fusion between organic and inorganic body.

In other words: "…the relation between organism and machine has been a border war. The stakes in the border war have been the territories of production, reproduction, and imagination. This [essay] is an argument for pleasure in the confusion of boundaries and for responsibility in their construction"[61].

A bit like Futurism, which tended towards "overturning" the system that preceded it, but applied to many social, political and geographical contexts, since it moved within the scope of the scheme, not that of the content.

Haraway, firmly rooted in materialist tradition, reminds us that to rethink the subject means rethinking its bodily roots.

For Foucault, as for Haraway, biotechnologies were a powerful indicator of the "desire to know" of the contemporary order of discourse. The discourse on modern technologies reveals not only the order of the scientific discourse that reigns in our society, but also the cultural imagination supporting it.

---

61   Donna Haraway, *op. cit.*, p. 22.

In this case, political subjectivity means women's ability to leave the identity mode connected with biological membership to take them to a relational level that puts at stake not only their relational capabilities, but also the ability to diverge from the physically located identity, to arrive at an identity constituted by an ongoing process to be found in the exchange on precise programmatic objects.

The Cyborg manifesto was a political transformation project. In common with the Manifestos of Futurism it had differing aspects: the belonging to a "minority" in rebellion, the cultural and far-sighted ability that the use of the latest technologies could be a way of liberation from the old domains, since there was no longer a power hierarchy; both for the novelty of the medium, and for the intimately democratic structure, or so it is said, of the technological means.

Haraway's Manifesto of 1988 is a look back at the past with a real plea for the contemporary, or is this merely the resounding delay of a century on a way of expressing thought patterns to exercise the power of the word in the Futurist manner?

The Futurist Manifesto of Lust

With the *Futurist Manifesto of Lust*, drawn up in Paris on 11 January 1913, the poetess Valentine de Saint-Point reappears. This continuation of the previous manifesto led her to express herself in a more direct, more provocative and more outrageous manner, using a term that is clearly on loan from religion, of a culturally negative slant, since it is one of the Seven Deadly Sins.

The first answer this time is openly addressed to public criticism collected from the previous manifesto: "A reply to those dishonest journalists who twist phrases to make the Idea seem ridiculous; to those women who only think what I have dared to say; to those for whom Lust is still nothing but a sin".

What de Saint-Point makes manifest is the energy of lust, the possibility that this be intended as a vital force, and that it be therefore known so well as to become a conscious potential and not a dark force, a vice. The capacity of the individual to give him- or herself to another with such force as to become oblivious, to be projected beyond the body to reach in two the unknown, creation, and sensuality.

The levelling that it makes of the three planes: physical, spiritual and intellectual, is observed as an unfolding of the dynamic forces which, only if all are capable of being fulfilled, can allow an individual achievement of completeness.

The discourse is complex and far deeper than it might seem at first sight through the *Manifesto of Lust*; it comes to recognize a dynamic and vital force for the individual[62].

Through this awareness, a woman can give herself to another as a transcendent act, a creative act of complete giving, thereby transcending any degree of vice, which always lurks in the corners generated by fear and ignorance, and rediscovering a capacity of living actively in the act of love and not enduring it.

Cruelty is the tearing of the veil of Maya which deprives women of the knowledge of their potential of total self-giving, in which they can find a part of their mutilated identity, to understand that only from the depths of their awareness can they find a new dignity and joy that is totally feminine. In order to constitute a strong and conscious individuality that might be equal to that of men.

A manifesto of emancipation that arguably finds more female issues, but which belongs to the emancipation of the individual regardless of gender: it implies the ability of self-giving and love, overcoming fears that let vice nest.

III.2.e *The Technical Manifesto of Futurist Literature*

"Sitting on the gas tank of an aeroplane, my stomach warmed by the pilot's head, I sensed the ridiculous inanity of the old syntax inherited from Homer."

The metaphor of the aircraft in which is immediate the idea of liberation from language is once again a double image, the sensation of lightness given by the flight is interwoven with the desire for linguistic freedom.

The temporality and the simultaneity of sensations and artistic solutions blend with the concreteness of life lived and the propeller of the aeroplane which gives the engine power and charges a communicative reality tamped by merely human expressive limits with objective necessity.

In short, it would seem that the aid of the machine was for Marinetti the best egress from the difficulties of language.

Expression is enriched by a means which, united with individual creativity, gives the opportunity to reach hybrid, unpredictable and mobile expressiveness as intellectual rapidity, on the one hand, and as precise and aseptic as the operation of an engine on the other.

---

62   Valentine de Saint-Point, *Manifesto della Lussuria*, 11 January 1913.

And the propeller added:

1. ONE MUST DESTROY SYNTAX AND SCATTER ONE'S NOUNS AT RANDOM, JUST AS THEY ARE BORN
2. ONE SHOULD USE INFINITIVES
3. ONE MUST ABOLISH THE ADJECTIVE
4. ONE MUST ABOLISH THE ADVERB
5. EVERY NOUN SHOULD HAVE ITS DOUBLE
6. ABOLISH EVEN THE PUNCTUATION
7. THERE IS AN EVER-VASTER GRADATION OF ANALOGIES, there are ever-deeper and more solid affinities, however remote.
8. THERE ARE NO CATEGORIES OF IMAGES. Therefore, the analogical style is absolute master of all matter and its intense life.
9. To render the successive motions of an object, one must render the chain of analogics that it evokes.
10. We must orchestrate images by arranging them according to a MAXIMUM DISORDER.
11. DESTROY THE *I* IN LITERATURE: that is, all psychology.

For Marinetti, there were three elements that would make up the new literature: 1. Sound (the dynamism of objects); 2. Weight (objects' faculty of flight); 3. Smell (objects' faculty of dispersing themselves).

The entire Futurist activity was to seize the dynamism of the newspaper and the artistic-literary disciplines made immobile: to mechanize every aspect of life and creativity, thus lifting the emotional side that burdens; using the fastest creations of the brain relating to the operation of machines, he theorized movement without affective Baroque-isms, free from psychological encumbrances, liberating and rewarding from a practical point of view. The operation of the mechanism of practical life applied to all fields of pleasure as well as artistic fields.

On 11 August 1912, he added a Supplement to the *Technical Manifesto of Futurist Literature*. In response to the criticisms and derogatory comments collected, Marinetti provided a more thorough explanation, one that was better-documented and more Futurist. He began by resting his thesis on two authoritative allies: Dante, with his XI Canto of *Paradise* and Edgar Allan Poe from *The Colloquy of Monos and Una*, both in verse against the reasoned explanation of intuitive art. The analogy is the logic of artistic creation and we cannot try to grasp it except through intuition and the lightness of the senses.

Punctuation is a logical ordering of the analogical path; thus, it must be eliminated. Joyce already had done so and was not worried about having to give an explanation, in this Marinetti had the wholly Italian concern of not being alone, of wanting to ensure that also others could understand, and this aspect made him paradoxically adherent to his own criticisms. Revealing the ideological side of his intentions.

CHAPTER IV

VI.1 *On Filippo Tommaso Marinetti*

The *Founding and Manifesto of Futurism* was published on 20 February 1909 in Paris, the European cultural centre of the early years of the Twentieth Century. Marinetti was living in Milan and the headquarters of the movement was in Via del Senato, 2: Marinetti's Home. Then, after 1925, he moved to Rome with his wife Benedetta.

The life and dissemination of Futurist art and theories required continuous movement, and Marinetti was in fact constantly travelling both around European cities[1]and throughout Italy.

Despite this, Futurism was present in every Italian region with different local exponents, all looking to Marinetti, however, each Futurism had developed its own characteristics.

Marinetti was therefore the reference for any hints of Futurism, from him came the idea of creating a movement around expressive needs, from him came the ability to organize and supply the Futurist idea around which would group the experimental artists of the early Twentieth Century.

Filippo Tommaso Marinetti was born in Alexandria in Egypt on 22 December 1876, his father Enrico Marinetti was a lawyer from Voghera, his mother, Amalia Grolli, the daughter of a professor of humanities, left her first husband imposed on her by her family, to marry Marinetti in a second marriage.

Both from a middle-class environment, they brought up their children in luxury albeit with solid bourgeois values such as the industriousness which Marinetti would translate literally from the bourgeois economic scheme to the cultural patterns he would seek to undermine.

---

1   "Marinetti passes half his life on a train: war correspondent and soldier in Tripoli, Benghazi and the Bulgarian trenches of Adrianople, Futurist propagandist in Paris, Brussels, Madrid, Moscow, Petrograd, Milan, and Palermo. His residence is the carriage", in B. Corra, E. Settimelli, *Marinetti Intimo* (Milan: Sonzogno, 1911).

His ideas were not then so original, it seems: the idea of the Manifestos had already been used by a group of French artists in 1907, *Compagnons de l'action d'art*, inspired by a fusion of anarchist and Nietzschean ideas. But in Italy this was something new, considering also the slowness of Italian culture in assimilating novelty which arose from its origins, this was generally facilitated when confirmed by international cultures, and from this point of view, Marinetti had the patriotism of the pre-war era and the cosmopolitanism of his Egyptian and French experience united with a grounding in Italian culture.

During his stay in Paris, Marinetti encountered all the new artistic theories and, on his return to Italy, gathered all those artists who were not recognized in the art of the country's institutions and who were looking for a recognition of their unusual way of feeling and expressing themselves.

Marinetti's theory followed all the steps necessary to establish an artistic canon that was an alternative to the classical one.

Marinetti's education was a classic one; he studied with the Jesuits in Alexandria, and graduated in Italy, almost exclusively through the will of his father, in Law.

His fate was in line with the plans of his family, to follow in the footsteps of his lawyer father, from whom he probably inherited a good oratorical capacity and an analysis of detail.

The second son after Leone, Tommaso remained an only child when he was about twenty, losing his brother as a result of heart disease.

The key idea to penetrate Marinetti's language is the primacy of the machine in the hierarchy of the passions of contemporary man, who no longer lost himself in the voluptuousness of women but was snared by the beauty of the speed of machines.

"We wanted to launch our race into a global conflagration. It was therefore necessary to heal it from excessive affectivity and nostalgia, exalting fast and distracted loves"[2]. But the machine was only half the story. The aim was to "awaken" the Italians.

The car was new to the point that there was still a debate in Italy over whether it was female or male, in fact, it was initially male.

It should be noted however that this cantor of the machine was not himself a motorist: after his first accident, he noted that his distraction did not make him a suitable candidate for driving and he was always to prefer the train for his travels, being driven by others, and even the horse carriage rather than the speed of the car which, although for him was an exalting source of fascination, he was unable to control without jeopardising his safety.

---

2   Filippo Tommaso Marinetti, *Marinetti e il Futurismo*, *op. cit.*, p. 620.

A considerable aporia; he who boasted of having discovered the new and more solid feeling of man with the machine and its progressive dependence on it, to replace it for the warm human body of a woman, in reality, did not make use of them at all.

The profile of Marinetti's character emerged clearly from his descriptions and his way of writing which was terse, immediate, and synthetic. A poem does not require a particularly elaborate construction to be such, the importance and the truthfulness of poetry or the work of art in general is given by its strength, this is the force present in the work of Marinetti: strength as energy, the compelling potential that is life, not reflection on it.

An idea that can be found in many ways in all innovators, revolutionaries and inventors of new languages, who have had the ability to open up new sensory universes to the world.

Marinetti was superstitious, perhaps an atavism from the country that gave him birth. He had his lucky number, eleven, and all of its multiples, he himself was born on 22 December and many decisions or representations were made on these days of the month.

He had delusions that were almost outrageous, such as the totally irrational idea that the mirror can be an object of ill omen, that together with the external image, it also captured the inner energy.

Marinetti declared that he had drawn up the Manifesto on 11 December 1908, but he seems to have waited for the new year, 1909, given that "it is not to be excluded that Marinetti thought 1909 a propitious year since he would be 33, a multiple of 11"[3].

The death of his Father Enrico at his home in Milan in Via Senato, 2, was to change only one thing: the mirror of the wardrobe had to be replaced by a drawing and from then on, his house would always be deprived of mirrors; it seems that even with his wife he was particularly careful that nothing happened to her pocket mirror.

The superstitions, analogical processes, and immediate intuitions explain the impetuous and seemingly unreasonable temperament of Marinetti, which was in many respects close to that of Mussolini, the intuitive force dominating over the educated reason of social schemes deemed to be surpassed.

---

3   Nico Stringa, *"...l'amato fecondo Manifesto": cenni sulla diffusione del Futurismo in Italia nel febbraio del 1909*, in "Futurismo. 1909-1944", (Milan: Mazzotta, 2001), pp. 195-209. Marinetti was born on 22 December; many manifestos are dated day 11; There are 11 points in the manifesto of the foundation of Futurism.

His contact with artists was very participatory and encouraging: a figure present with continuous letters, postcards, telegrams, all of his activities aimed at a quick contact, his presence essential, not too awkward but at the same time a continuous incitement to the moral frustrations or depressions that artists encounter.

In the correspondence between Marinetti and Palazzeschi the relationship was clearly intimate; Palazzeschi demonstrated a sincere friendship towards him, perhaps because he felt encouraged in his original talent for the first time, Marinetti by his use of very formal tones, through which he seemed to want to nourish the trust of the twenty-five-year-old Palazzeschi.

"You can't wait, you're so keen, come..," wrote Marinetti in a letter of 1910. The day after he wrote, "Come, we absolutely need you."

A further field to investigate is the question of Futurism with respect to women. In observing Marinetti's actions, what he says of women should be read with the eyes of his impetuosity, his contempt for women which he often said was to be contextualized with the code of the time, the contempt for *that* woman, the type of woman that *that* time and *those* contingencies produced: a woman who was languid, suffering because defenceless, incapable of reacting to her own position of unconscious submission, also prevented in her action by the role she bore as a container of sentiment, who revealed herself in the light of futurist actions and writings as a development phase of human sensibility.

The woman as a social product of that period had certain precise characteristics: immobility, weakness, sentimentality, and the fact of attacking and unmasking her so publicly lets us understand that the new sought by Marinetti involved all the categories and social roles of the erstwhile heritage. He seems to have wanted to empower and encourage female emancipation from the usual roles.

In his descriptions of women is found a powerful ability to find in each her own beauty, even in those details that were generally not socially used to define female beauty:

"Gorgeous young ladies, all black penetrating eyes and shading of whiskers on the upper lip. Sensuality, grace and elegance"[4].

The beauty of the woman is here clearly defined by what these ladies emanate from their energies rather than by their more or less moustached appearance, even the whisker assumes its poetic, and perhaps downplaying quality.

---

4   Filippo Tommaso Marinetti, *Taccuini 1915/1921* (Bologna: il Mulino, 1987).

The end of Futurism's innovative vein dates for some scholars of the movement to 1914, while for others it can be prolonged until 1919.

The magazine was the main tool to disseminate Futurism, the entire work of the movement was written about in magazines; responses to provocations that came from conferences, to quarterly publications, and letters written between them to leave room in the magazines.

Marinetti's work was explosive in that it was served with instruments which made its publication explosive; he would not have been able to achieve the same scope by writing a book. Moreover, Futurism was against the book, but even here the interpretation cannot be literal because the language was used with another code of meanings.

The book, like the woman, stood for the concept the word led to, the book itself revealed a conception of life, a hierarchy of possibilities, a reverent fear of the past, for what had been said, lived, processed in another time and hence, as such, it restricted access except through our quality as interpreters.

The Futurists tried to steal their capability of interpretation without wishing to pass via the education of how works were conceived in their genesis, claiming an alleged innate personal capacity of individuals to have their own autonomous interpretative apparatus dictated by personal experience.

But the weakness of this presumption was in contradiction with the complexity of the work, which always arose from a social context, from an individual life, and ultimately entered the lived experience of a spectator/reader.

Also in this case, the book, like the woman, and like the past itself, was not demonized in its essence, it was its crystallized meaning that was to be challenged and destroyed.

In 1909, Marinetti sent a letter to Papini to discover what he thought of the publication of the Manifesto. The latter considered himself an anti-Futurist and he himself admitted that he judged the Futurists a movement of artists for the most part exalted and of little value, if only for their transitive property of so much fuss in so little substance.

It was specified with determination that his response would be published in *Poesia*, the Futurist magazine that Marinetti had created and now edited.

We can see Papini gradually coming intellectually into line with the Futurist findings: Marinetti wrote a letter to him in 1913 to vent his spleen over Apollinaire's alleged plagiarism of the Futurist thesis, without however confessing his paternity. He became overheated over this deception even though his main purpose was to export the Futurist revolution throughout Europe, as revealed by his travels to Russia, to London, and around France and Spain.

Marinetti would always vindicate the primacy of Futurist theory over all the avant-garde movements that developed subsequently: Dadaism, Surrealism, and Cubo-Futurism in Russia.

But this primacy of the need to change the artistic language, by progressively investing it with a growing political power, was identified as a bourgeois revolution for its extreme rush to power.

According to several scholars, Futurism was none other than bourgeois art trying to change its codes, it was no coincidence that it was bourgeois sensibility that had enabled it to cross the threshold of its own limits and exert power over the Socialist advance.

The birth of an artistic movement that took place via the official publication of its ideological intent, announced the tone that would be maintained in all subsequent publications until the end of the movement on the death of its chief entrepreneur and designer.

However, the fact was that other movements had already used this type of advertising tool to announce their presence.

The Futurist Manifesto had disclosed all its power for the first time in *Le Figaro* on 22 December 1909, since the alternative art whose values it bore needed to "signal its presence in an environment that was not only artistic since it would have died immediately, the short-sighted view of the art critics would have nipped in the bud any innovative intent that was not purely artistic in the classic way."

Marinetti took his time, and announced an idea of art before it could be killed off by the official institutions with the accusation of precariousness or an inability to comply with the usual canons of art.

Thus, the advertising gimmick became a perfect expedient for something imminent that was not yet ready in its final draft and did not intend to offer itself as finished art, but demanded continuous progress from itself, a continuous elaboration, thereby condemning itself to insecurity with its declaration of being able and willing to last no more than ten years.

Marinetti perceived the instability of the modern world and embodied and straddled it, demanding from his artists, rapidity, dedication, passion, speed and nimbleness, with the awareness of someone who knew that he stood at the beginning of a process of change which was so radical and slow in its evolution that it used itself as a tool and did not attempt to cling to the eternity of the work and the word, thus going down in history in every respect.

In Marinetti's letters to Cangiullo, the one constant was the encouragement he gave the artist. Urging him to write more quickly, re-correcting some things, emphasizing others, his attitude took the form of a modeller of expressiveness. The few works or poems that he rejected were those devoid of inner strength, regardless of the expressive modalities employed.

It is evident that the Futurist work tried to shift sensibility rather than communicate a transcendence in art; in this phenomenon, art became the instrument to bring sensibility to the fore, with artists and works that might never have managed to reach such a resonance.

In some ways, we can say that Futurism gave voice to what had never been heard, except through communication strategies. And its strength was precisely in having identified the movement in a manner strictly correlated to the society of consumption: the work lasted no more than ten years, human sensibility was renewed and multiplied by the very speed of the ideas, it was sufficient to tune in to the production of ideas and the time for their realization, the productive mechanism that served to produce a design object. The idea, the project, and the timeframes that production tools could offer.

However, thanks to the intrinsic law of contradiction that characterized Futurism, this artistic action was needed in society, but in the venues of the avant-garde and therefore disengaged from the social rules. In dialectic with society, but one step ahead of it.

VI.2 _The Futurist Debate on Journals_

The meeting of Marinetti with Croce was certainly not lacking in profound criticism on the part of the philosopher; for him Futurism was neither art nor poetry, and from his point of view, not without reason; "... the great industry of the void", was Croce' judgement of the avant-garde.

Not entirely beyond dispute, the Futurist intention was not to create art but to create a new sensibility, which did not exclude that it was an impalpable creation, and in certain respects a creation of the void.

But what analogy connected things so deeply different? In this case, a cultured man with a Jesuit education, soaked in legal studies (also through the legacy of a lawyer father), who, in love with his homeland, like all of those who had lived it in an idealized way, wanted to liberate it through creative transgression.

In fact, Marinetti's was a life of constant movement, he would travel from one end of the country to the other and throughout Europe to divulge his idea, his theory that dominated everyday life, forgetting however to have contact with what he said: he proclaimed a life of experience and not of study, but because he knew study more seriously, in some way he rejected everything he had obtained from his privileged position, taking advantage of it in his own favour and wreaking havoc in a social and economic situation in which he understood he could only take part by working from the outside.

His was a position of privilege: the Parisian period had enriched his most important knowledge from an artistic point of view, and he returned to Italy with clear ideas, awakened the Italians from their torpor and inserted them in the European cultural debate.

But he fought against the cultural conflicts inside his own country, and initially even the intellectual anarchists rejected him. Papini himself would take several years and various disappointments before becoming involved in the Futurist impulse which moved on the desperate conviction of explaining truths to a nation that were not yet accessible to it.

Marinetti professed the life he could and wanted to afford, the modernism of his lifestyle in contact with the entire world, frantic departures, hurried human contacts but attentive to the intellectual detail, by their very nature rapid, that took shape in his manifestos.

In reality, Futurism must be observed through the eyes of the correspondence, witticisms and answers in magazines, while the cultural debate was supported and most of the information and opinions were contained in the articles of the anarchist or anti-academic monthlies such as *Leonardo*, *Lacerba*, *Poesia*, and *La Voce*.

The magazine *Lacerba* was born out of the necessity of Papini and Soffici to separate from Prezzolini's magazine, *La Voce*, which had become less and less open to international artistic needs, and thus create a magazine for the literary avant-garde.

The two intellectuals already came from different experiences of magazines with revolutionary content. They had been part of the first nucleus of young anarchists who met in November 1902 to give life to the magazine *Leonardo*, which was to bring together a mixture of intellectuals and artists, including painters such as Adolfo de Karolis, John Costetti, Paul Mussini, and Armando Spadini, and poets and writers such as Alfredo Bona, Macinai Ernesto and Mario Venturini.

The birth of *Leonardo* originated from a need for new spaces and fewer restrictions both in terms of context and topics.

The first series of *Leonardo* closed in May 1903 in a considerable muddle of ideas and aspirations. The editorial staff dispersed and the new core of Papini and Prezzolini redesigned the magazine in a substantially different way.

The first *Leonardo* had been ephemeral in its composition, but the second series was based on solidly intellectual logic, and brought together names such as Maffio Maffii, Marcello Taddei and De Karolis[5].

The new format of the magazine was successful, and a third series was planned which, by 1907, appeared to be bogged down in esoteric and occultist conceptions.

The impossibility for an intellectual like Papini to endorse his new circle of companions such as Roberto Assagioli, the founder of Psychosynthesis, Aldo De Rinaldis and Arturo Reghini, meant that he decided on the demise of his own magazine with a farewell article entitled *La Fine – "The End"* – in which we read:

> Three times we welcomed different men and three times we had to recognize the impossibility of the blends. The first marriage was with logicians, mathematicians and analysts, who became intolerable for their lack of tolerance and for their inability to understand the artistic and adventurous side of our work; and the third with occultists from whom, after the last number, we definitively separated. [...] Today, out of the respect we owe to our own souls, we feel the need to sink this boat that was so expensive for us. [...] They try, if possible (those who followed it), to look at themselves as others could look at them, and if they could consider themselves without disgust, then even *Leonardo* will not have died in vain.[6]

Bitter and crude the words of Papini who, the blunt intellectual he had already demonstrated to be several times, was unable to admit the transformation of the magazine without first destroying it.

In this his attitude was deeply rigorous and Futurist, leading him with the publication in 1912 of *Un Uomo Finito* to put an end to his crisis that may have begun with the end of *Leonardo*.

In a brotherly friendship with Soffici, he regained his vigour in *La Voce* until once again he had to admit difficulty in his relations with Prezzolini, and left, together with Soffici, to found the new magazine *Lacerba*[7].

---

5   Alberto Viviani, *Origini del Nuovo Spirito Italiano* (Rome: Tosi, 1942).
6   Giovanni Papini, *Il mio Futurismo*, Second Edition with an additional essay Contro Florence Passatista 9° migliaio. (Florence: Edizioni di "Lacerba", 1914).
7   A. Viviani, *op. cit.*

Ardengo Soffici, he too by now in crisis with the editorial staff of *La Voce* was the inventor and coordinator of the new magazine which gradually became a venue for intense discussions and defence in favour of the avant-garde. The greatest personalities involved in the artistic debate, such as Palazzeschi, Ungaretti, Boccioni, Carrà, and Marinetti, would join the magazine.

Lacerba ran from 1 January 1913 to 22 May 1915. Born as a magazine of the artistic and literary avant-garde, it was to suddenly change its approach with the fluctuating political situation. The crisis and the impending war decided the fate of the editorial staff: as the publisher, Vallecchi intervened directly by writing a letter to Soffici and Papini with a proposal to transform the magazine from artistic and literary commitment to political commitment. Papini responded enthusiastically to this proposal and *Lacerba* soon became the official organ of Italian Interventionism.

The magazine was immediately successful, and Papini became the organizer of the new format. In number 6, year 1 of *Lacerba*, dated 15 March 1913, an article by Papini appeared on the first page entitled *Contro il Futurismo* (*Against Futurism*), in which he initially presented himself as an intellectual outside the membership of any group, least of all Futurism.

With the same authority as an intellectual observer of his country's political, social and cultural movements, he revealed in this article his progressive cultural approach to the motivations of Futurism. Emphasizing his fundamental distance from many initiatives of the movement, he presented himself as open to considering Futurist actions in relation to their willingness to communicate new principles, and new relations between the artist and society.

In this, Papini saw the need for communication of the artist who continuously creates situations of turmoil to invoke consideration; to ensure that his or her work is implemented as an expression, and that through the tool of writing, painting, theatre, sculpture, or these arts mixed together, does not appreciate aesthetic communication so much as expressive necessity as the symbol of a need for new codes.

A need no different from the circle of anarchists with whom Papini set up the magazine in continuous controversy with Italy's culture of hegemony.

In this context, art became less sacred, became a "virtual" communication of human experience, and as such demanded a response from its peers, and especially demanded to hear with its own ears, and probably also to be able to personally rebut, the praises or even the boos directed at it.

Art demanded consideration, and when closing his article Papini revealed that these young people, although not always able to create new works, or to be as brilliant as they would like, nonetheless demonstrated the desire to innovate, to experience new principles and innovative ways of making art, making contemporary art more socialized.

With his infectious energy, Marinetti also won over the most caustic intellectual of the time, converting him to the cause of expressiveness against the codification of expressive codes to the detriment of communication.

In other words, it was not a different battle they were fighting, merely with different weapons and on several fronts.

The experience of previous publishing issues opened Papini's intellectualism to the awareness of a search on several fronts.

In reality, Marinetti's activity was neither full of aestheticism like the artists who congregated around *Hermes*, the magazine born from the first break-up of *Leonardo*, nor did he appropriate the right of awareness through calculating reason; he was the spokesperson of a quality that summarized and synthesized the balance of these two faculties: *Instinct*.

And it was precisely "instinct" that was the only guide in traversing unfamiliar situations. In the new century, with its use of the machine, individuals had to transform their rhythms, their habits of life and swap old certainties for the unknown.

Marinetti believed he could find the solution in instinct, indicated as the sapiential capacity to live and experience first-hand, which trained the senses and accustomed one's sense of danger.

Danger was the unknown, the machine was the new that was unknown. And only the individual instinctively searching for life could relate to it successfully.

In a letter dated 4 July 1914, Marinetti wrote to Papini asking him to publish a manifesto on the first page of the 15 July issue of *Lacerba*. Vallecchi was the publisher of the manifestos and Marinetti asked for 6,000 copies to be shipped, of which for the moment he had only received 400 copies, and he begged Papini to put him directly in touch with Vallecchi.

In another undated letter, Marinetti sent a manifesto to Papini that he wanted published in *Lacerba*. This was a manifesto that continued the movement's artistic action using it and transforming it into political action.

In the meantime, Giovanni Papini had published *Il Mio Futurismo,* a booklet bound in a reddish-purple cover, in which he spent time describing in detail and point by point the reasons and mode of his approach to the most discussed movement of the time, which was also the most intellectually unbecoming.

This approach cost Papini no little criticism on the part of the contemporary cultural elite, and he himself prepared to give notice, evolution and explanation of it: he specified that his position was not dictated by any turnaround as he was wrongly accused of, in view also of the renowned roughness of his character, and he testified that he had read a large part of the Futurist production albeit with a little initial difficulty.

He freely confessed the difficulty of approach that he himself had in reading the Futurist works, and then said he could understand especially "delicate palates" that associated acrobats, village fêtes and coarse circus events with noise, and that all of this made reception of Futurist production impenetrable, beyond their message.

The volume opened in this way: "Italian Futurism has made people laugh, yell and spit. Let us see if it might make people think"[8].

In this case, the medium really was the message, in the words of McLuhan, who allegedly remarked that Marinetti was a not very scientifically lucid precursor.

Returning to the motivations of validity of the message that the Futurists provided through their manifestos, theatrical evenings, and travelling exhibitions, Papini said that at the sight of the first Futurist manifesto he had finally the good news/surprise that someone was attempting something new, something that "celebrates temerity and violence and stands for freedom and destruction!", and he added:

> it is a pity, however, that they feel the need to write with such emphasis, with these seventeenth-century notions barely masked by the mechanical, and that they present themselves with the air of tragic clowns who want to frighten the placid spectators of a matinee at an outdoor cinema. It could be rawer and stronger without making as much racket!

In reality, Papini recognized in this "Futurist racket" an anarchist version applied to art, although his concerns were linked to the choice of proclaiming manifestos, which was related to previous Parisian ones, among which for example the manifesto of the group of artists called *"Compagnons de l'action d'art"* who, with a manifesto of 1907, may have introduced the idea of artistic theory advertised via manifestos, with poor results and unfortunately revealing the scaffolding of an advertising not backed up by a validity of content to be transmitted.

---

8   G. Papini, *op. cit.*

The 'form' of Futurism strikes and unsettles those accustomed to a certain refined and simple 'good taste', which is not – for goodness' sake! – the coldness of classicisms but can be found together as a natural form, with a forwardness and cynicism of thought equal to at least that of the most frenetic Futurists.[9]

The intentions of the movement were coherent with Papini's own ideas, just a few pages later, he proclaimed himself an unconscious Futurist, having published in 1905 *Il Crepuscolo dei Filosofi*, "...which I could well have called a Futurist philosophy essay".

Two aspects of Futurism prevented less adventurous intellectuals from accepting the arguments of the new movement:

a) the Futurists debuted with a manifesto that recalled the interventions of previous French artistic failures;

b) The Futurists were destroyers in words but lenient in action, which made them scarcely credible and clearly revealed their bourgeois origins.

Essentially, Papini was attracted by Futurism because it was such a strong, addictive movement, that sought freedom through oddities, felt itself akin to an outpouring of "redemption" but remained in reality quite far from Marinetti's formal personality, even though in the years between '14 and '15 there would be a flurry of letters between them: in 1909, Marinetti had already asked Papini for his judgement on the Futurist Manifesto and whether his affiliation would be total or partial. Papini's answer, Marinetti announced, would be published in *Poesia*[10].

In a letter dated October 1913, Marinetti wrote to Papini that because of his public conferences, it was vital that there be an understanding between art and politics for a change in attitude to bring a glimmer of light to the new minds and new artistic possibilities and then added: "There are many idiots but there are also many lively minds waiting to express their ideas." He requested that an article be published in *Lacerba* dealing with art and politics.

Papini recognized the courage of these young intellects even though he did not praise their creations at all; while, as regards Marinetti, his consideration was that it was enough to ensure that the union with the impetus of this Milanese's revolt brought momentum to his magazine and its unfulfilled anarchist sentiment.

---

9   Cfr. G. Papini, *op. cit.*

10   Cfr. Archivio Papini, Marinetti-Papini letters, Centro Documentazione Avanguardie Storiche Primo Conti, "Le Coste", Fiesole.

On the death of Marinetti, in 1944, Papini's diary of 4 December reads:

News has come that F.T. Marinetti, the founder of Futurism has died in Milan. He was born in 1876. I met him in 1913; and although I was linked to him – for a brief time – by literary reasons and polemics, I never liked him and there was never a true friendship between us. He was too different in character and origin from me. His motto could be the title of Shakespeare's comedy: *Much Ado About Nothing*. D'Annunzio defined him as 'a phosphorescent cretin'. Petrolini perfected the definition like this: a cretin with splashes of idiocy. Definitions that are too strict. In truth, this was a too-American D'Annunzio and a too-serious Petrolini. One of his teachers was Barnum; one of his disciples Mussolini.[11]

The collaboration between Futurism and Papini's magazine began in 1913, and was substantially a collaboration more concerned with the means of the magazine than common intent, Papini convinced himself little by little, particularly for the swiftness and perhaps also the topicality of the movement, however, he never fully espoused the Futurist cause. He did not share the same motivation; his anarchic battle was ultimately very personal and he saw the team spirit of the Futurists as a dangerous grouping that could impoverish the spirit. He always took care not to join the group and had a heated controversy with Boccioni that was rapid-fire precisely because of his absolute inability to feel an uncritical part of the group.

Futurist production announced with simplicity and dryness that art was a product of the human spirit that created another material: "Thanks to turning away in search of ever greater novelties its autonomous possibilities seem to be depleted. We are facing the raw material. The circle closes. Art returns reality; thought gives itself up to action," and in addition: "Have we really dried up all the sources of personal creativity to meet the abdication of means that are really artistic and our own?"[12].

Umberto Boccioni responded to the provocation with an article of 1 March 1914 that reinforced the motivations of Futurism and the principles which impelled it to search for new tools: the means handed down from history were exhausted and unsuitable for the expression of emotions aroused by the new conditions of life, science had transformed the dimensions of reality and to be able to receive and reconvert these stimuli

---

11   Giovanni Papini, *Diario* (Florence: Vallecchi, 1962).
12   Giovanni Papini, *Il cerchio si chiude*, 15 February 1914, "Archivi del Futurismo" (Rome: De Luca, 1962), p. 190.

into artistic expressions demanded a radical free experimentation in all possible fields of communication[13].

Papini's response reflected his allergy to groups, "on entering Futurism I did not think I was entering a church but a group of revolutionary and unscrupulous artists who sought destruction and originality above all else"[14].

In reality, Papini's provocation was more a request for an explanation with regard to the experimental Futurist constructions, rather than a real targeted criticism: as an intellectual, Papini could recognize the originality and the revolutionary ways of the movement but could not grasp the potential evolution and artistic continuity, above all he asked whether this type of art or this type of violent rush towards the future might not "lead someone to specks of Verismo that were crazier than the old Verismo"[15].

The debate here was ongoing and concrete, and Papini's critical acumen observed the Futurist movement and stressed its basic lack of critical judgement: the group was extremely cohesive, the artists enjoying a protection that allowed them the most unbridled freedom without the spectrum of non-acceptance; art was accepted as energy and vibration, and criticisms or external judgements might well not undermine its creative serenity.

---

13   Umberto Boccioni, *Il cerchio non si chiude*, in "Lacerba", 1 March 1914.
14   Giovanni Papini, *Cerchi aperti*, in "Lacerba", 15 March 1914.
15   *Ibid*.

CONCLUDING REMARKS:
THE ARTISTIC ACTION AS SOCIAL CRITIQUE

Marinetti's idea of disclosing and imposing a rereading of reality according to the Futurist interpretation of history and tradition, revealed a conception of art that had become an instrument to influence reality and the perception of it.

This creative act was not an alternative to social action, but constituted an extension of it. The foundations on which the interpretation of reality by science and culture rested had reached their explicit formulation by the early Twentieth Century. Thus, it would be up to the subsequent one to spread Freud's theories showing all the frailty of the conceptual elaborations that were considered anchored to the prerequisites of an unassailable rationalism.

The discovery of the unconscious as a profound primary motor of action and the organization of reality, as well as an inexhaustible source of energy, in the Surrealists found a space in need of a deep knowledge of interiority and its expressions; in Futurism, instead, there was an attempt to shift the awareness of the individual from the human condition as acceptance, to the desire to work on the given reality.

On the one hand, the awareness of the unconscious and its instincts had introduced doubt about events as such, on the other, it had induced a hypertrophy of the "I" that deceived the individual into holding inordinate power over history and human destiny. History itself then lost that linearity so dear to the Enlightenment, at the basis of the "religion" of progress, and arose as a magmatic, multi-directional process that did not "have a libretto", to coin Isaiah Berlin's phrase.

In the idea of progress as a chronological fatality, what prevailed was the disquieting awareness of an essential hardship. The artistic experience became the way out of the crisis of reason.

Through the creative acceptance of a given reality, prismatic in its meanings, a search was made for the meaning of contemporaneity. A coexistence of contradictions and explanations, theories and inventions that indicated a dialectic between external and internal, between society and individuals aware of their mutual influences, but who attempted a solution in the absorption of reality as it presented itself and in its creative elaboration drawn from the depths of the new energy of the individual and society.

One through self-knowledge, the other through the production and exploitation of energy.

In Futurist production, subjectivity and objectivity intersected, they overlapped until losing their identity in one another.

In this perspective, Futurism gave rise to extraordinary advances. It carried out the first virtual acts, it had the maximum ambition of being able to shape reality with the force of the imagination and the mind, it created that "virtual reality" which is talked about so much today, the word "avant-garde" in this sense began to assume a different connotation: an avant-garde of the future approach to life.

Social changes would work extensively on both the relational and dialogical capacity of action in reality and a sense of history on the part of the individual.

The avant-garde anticipated the expressive plane, but was unable to cope with the logic of bureaucratic development.

The logics clashed: the logic of creative solutions for the survival of the vital energy went against the logic of the organization that tended to maintain the order of a bureaucratic type needed to operate the system.

This breakdown pre-announced not only the fragmentation or speed of the modern era, but also the virtual action, the invented and cathartic fact that marked standardized lives.

The creative act of which I spoke at the beginning was therefore the ability to give life to a context within the context, the artistic work; both the possibility of confounding the historical fact and confounding reality as a defence against impotence.

But there was a third aspect generated by the creative act as a virtual act: the new datum of experience born from the communication of a fact and not necessarily from its physical and material presence. Anticipation not merely as a prophecy, but as a future act that acted on the present retrospectively, and thus with far from predictable feedback. An active negation.

Max Weber had stated that the meaning of an action consisted in the sense that the actor attached to it, to the project pursued through this act, but in this he neglected the necessary gap that existed between the lived and its immediacy.

The attribution of sense given by the project as anticipation, was always different from its retrospective realization. Total identification between the lived and reflection on the lived experience was never given, and certainly not on the perception that third parties had of this same experience. There was always a tension between the two moments[1].

The consequence was that, in agreement with Weber's claim, the same action could be attributed different meanings depending on the point of view the interpretation of it began from, *a posteriori*.

This critical instance inserted by A. Schütz in the theory of social action is interesting if applied to the avant-garde, since it allows us to observe the avant-garde Futurist project both as a futuristic anticipation and as a later practical influence of a specific reality on the historical plane. The action of contemporary art would then arise as an action that anticipated, hence a project, to be realized in the present as art, however, and only subsequently as social action.

Therefore, the ridge along which social and artistic action moved saw them united in the avant-garde act, the anticipator of a project of change in organization and social relations, but at the same time the historical situation blocked them and only let them live in an imaginary or fantastic-artistic context.

The creative act thus assumed a key position in the society of the day: it operated on capitalist society precisely in virtue of its total dedication to non-utilitarian expression. It created a vacuum between functionality and its direct abutment in the social fabric.

Because of this it became retroactive. By doing away with the subject, Futurism created an emotional impact that affected reactivity: it broke down, multiplied and confused the forms, became lost in history because of voluntarily losing contact with it in its total tension towards the future.

Life began to follow a destructured, virtual flow. This mode of action could be partly considered among those non-logical actions of which Pareto spoke, since actions not corresponding to a connection of the logical type with respect to social conventions were nonetheless likely to be active in contexts that may not have been official but were socially determinant for change.

The revolution in the role of art through the work of the historical avant-garde schools of Impressionism, Cubism, Expressionism, Futurism, Surrealism, Vorticism and Rayonism, affirmed the new cultural entity active in society.

Above all, the artistic action seems to have reached its greatest expressions with precisely this art that quickly burned out its potential, that

---

1   Alfred Schütz, *Saggi Sociologici* (Turin: UTET, 1979), p. IX.

did not form schools, and left the legacy of an artistic process rather than expressive canons to be adopted or surpassed.

This innovation affected the making of art and not the work itself. Certainly, form is the tangible result of artistic work, and with Futurism it found the first signs of abstraction, but it also found the first experiments with the fusions of several materials, expressions belonging to different planes of reality: sight, touch, smell, and hearing. "The coinciding of the institution and the content of the works was the logical condition of development that allowed the avant-garde to question art."[2].

The consideration of E. Jünger that "when something alien appears on the horizon, moreover in unusual amounts and proportions, it cannot be mere coincidence. Thus, we correctly ask ourselves about the links"[3], was a key reference in the motivation behind this research.

At this point, we could say that the prophecy of the avant-garde prefigured the changing role of art in society, the growing need for expression in everyday life, the discovery of an internal dynamism in each practice, the progressive closure of the possibility for the individual to live in the present, the possibility in art of freeing the individual from the need to be "functional" which the capitalist organization imposed for social integration. The possibility of finding one's own way to straddle contemporaneity through a creative act.

Art becoming necessity.

Futurism decomposed forms in their dynamism. In this sense, the prophetic significance of this movement adopted a supra-personal and supra-artistic objective, became the guiding thread of history that inspired a rereading of the moments of maximum irrationality as stages in the expansion of knowledge.

Propaganda, the presence of journalism, and advertising hype brought forward at all levels of cultural communication gave the phenomenon of Futurism a popularity and self-definition without precedents in the history of artistic movements. The Self changed position and launched communicative representation.

In substance, the avant-garde defined its own self-perception as reality, without waiting for this perception to be assimilated and transformed by the context that welcomed it. It wanted to change the perception of the context, not to belong to it.

---

2   Peter Bürger, *Teoria dell'avanguardia* (Turin: Bollati Boringhieri, 1990), p. 59.
3   Ernst Jünger, *Al muro del Tempo* (Milan: Adelphi, 2000), p. 12.

Self-representation as avant-garde was the turning point of contemporary art, which anticipated a social dynamic of social integration with an interpersonal mode typical of the contemporary context. But "the new firstly requires sacrifice, since it not only wants to occupy the space already inhabited, but also wants to be deserved, earned, and conquered. On the arrival of the new an acclimation followed, with discomfort, fevers and epidemics, and even death"[4], and in this sense the need for a life capable of transcending social limitations and regaining its ability to act concretely was part of the struggle of almost all avant-garde movements.

The destruction of the values of the past and especially the refusal of any continuity with previous history made the re-foundation of new values possible.

The interruption of the traditional logical constraint, with the risk of irrationalism, laid the foundations for a new mode of logic: the abolition of the hierarchies.

Did the separation from citizen-institutions not perhaps have its origin in a dissection of the social reality that the avant-garde schools had already denounced in their repudiation of museums, academies and institutions?

Behind the irrational drive of avant-garde art were the new responsibilities of the artist which indicated, since an individual was partially external to the social organization of production, that if the institutions no longer served the individual, these did not fulfil their function and frustrated their existence.

The slowness of the work by hand against the speed of the machine, its perfection and its "technical reproducibility", activated a sense of omnipotence in the human soul which, allied with total confidence in scientific research, hence the totally human and controllable matrix, initiated a wave of rational enthusiasm devoid of reasonableness.

Although the Futurist man was represented as Mafarka, a god of himself who alone could manipulate destiny, in Futurism the sense of mystery was never abandoned, the mystical tension remained, except that it found alternative roads for its fulfilment.

It sought to eliminate all the structures that had become simulacra devoid of interactive possibilities, in favour of a society which, using the machine, wove more extensive webs of relationships.

Individuals were "in a relationship", only in this way could they be constituted as subjects, the avant-garde movements had seen the extension of the relationship of the subject with the outside through all the languages of technique and expression.

---

4   *Ibid.*, p. 13.

A further interpretation might be to observe the avant-garde movements as symptoms of a search for human meaning that desperately tried to escape mere market logic: this was the utopia of the avant-garde which ended, like real utopias, in pieces. But that gave, through those pieces, suggestions of "other" ways of life, from which new social dimensions and habitats often arose.

The historical discontinuity created by the Industrial Revolution, the passage from a society based on the ideals of primary need to ideals of practicality and gain, constituted the presuppositions of modernity.

In the modern era, ever-more efficient energy masses became available. Energy was the new presence in Futurist Art.

The Freudian discovery of the unconscious, when it helped to reveal repressed memory and then dominate it, put vital new energies at the disposal of individuals who were thus released from their crippling taboos.

There is no question that with industrialization, energy is no longer natural, but has been technically multiplied – from coal to oil, from electricity to electronics, to the atom. This was the underground protagonist of the new social condition, giving birth to acceleration, industrial production, quantities that exceeded daily need and that risked, as Marx had correctly foreseen, breaking the short circuit between overproduction and under consumption.

Avant-garde art worked on institutions by claiming to be a part of the ideological act to educate sensibility, and on the other hand, in a contradictory manner, to re-educate to freedom of expression and passion, to outdo the institutions, which was in itself a revolutionary act.

In this way, the concept of creativity seemed to move from an artistic dimension to a daily dimension, may even have transformed many everyday actions into extraordinary ones; perhaps the nucleus of aggregation of the new society fit precisely into this possibility of individuals to experience action as creative in every area of their existence.

Observing the creative act as an opening towards a possible reality was a more sophisticated way of observing society.

Social change always occurs because of several contributing issues, the movements of several factors, but this change must be interpreted appropriately in order to constitute a source of knowledge.

The dimension of the artistic action was also the fruit of a series of social phenomena and historical dynamics. Art was an observation of reality with eyes that revealed brand-new connections: it had codes, relationships, meanings in dialogue with certain aspects of society that were never the same at the same time.

The historical avant-garde, especially Futurism and Surrealism, promoted a global ideology, inspired by "collective myths" in a project that extended far beyond aesthetic innovations, the intervention was directly in politics, in the social life and in customs. They tried to create a culture that went beyond culture, which would be able to understand the "objective contradictions of the social process in its becoming historical"[5], by directing the art revolution as a need for the enlargement of visual culture.

In line with cultural studies, we are outlining a new ground battle: the new wars are psychic, virtual, of opposing mentalities, also because by now cultures are no longer local.

The Futurist movement can be considered as an organism. Or better, a complex phenomenon which, through some conceptual categories that synthesized it, such as social activism, speed, progress, analogy, territorial relativity, opened the way to a new social act: "A human praxis that appropriates social relations, social structures, internalizes and reprocesses them in psychological structures for its activity of destructuring-restructuring. Every human life is revealed from its less generalizable aspects as a vertical synthesis of a social history"[6]; a non-logical action that acted according to the criterion of the fragment, the daily, and that could become, from a culture of fragmentation of the psyche, a culture that integrated plurality in growth, without assimilating it.

In this sense, we can speak of Futurism as an attempt to overcome the present which, through the anticipation of history, formulated a prophecy by driving and filling the social imagination in a period of robust growth of irrationality.

With the expressive responsibility of those who, from the avant-garde, broke the lines of tradition to observe the enemy more closely, subdividing and fragmenting the old artistic form with a utopian impetus of reconstruction and the re-foundation of society with new values glimpsed far off in the distance.

---

5   Franco Ferrarotti, *Lineamenti di storia del pensiero sociologico* (Rome: Donzelli, 2002), p. 372.

6   Franco Ferrarotti, *Storia e storie di vita,* II° ed., (Bari-Rome: Laterza, 1995), p. 4.

BIBLIOGRAPHY

Sociology and Philosophy

Theodor W. Adorno, *Aesthetic Theory* (Minneapolis: University of Minnesota Press, 1997).

Theodor W. Adorno, Max Horkheimer, *Lezioni di Sociologia* (Turin: Einaudi, 1966-2001).

Hannah Arendt, *Sulla Violenza* (Parma: Guanda, 1996).

Rudolph Arnheim, *Arte e Percezione Visiva* (Milan: Feltrinelli, 1962).

Alain Badiou, The Century (Cambridge: Polity, 2007)

Walter Benjamin, *Arte e rivoluzione*, It. transl., (Turin: Einaudi, 1972).

Peter L. Berger, Thomas Luckmann, *The Social Construction of Reality: A treatise in the sociology of knowledge* (New York: Random House, 1966).

Marshall Berman, *All that is Solid Melts into Air. The Experience of Modernity* (London: Penguin Books, 1988).

Antoine Compagnon, *Les cinq paradoxes de la modernité* (Paris: Seuil, 1990).

Enrico Castelnuovo, *Arte, Industria, Rivoluzioni* (Turin: Einaudi, 1985).

Franco Crespi, *Teoria dell'agire sociale* (Bologna: il Mulino, 1999).

Franco Crespi, *Manuale di sociologia della cultura* (Rome-Bari: Laterza, 1996).

Franco Ferrarotti, *Arte e società*, in "De Homine", (Rome, 1960).

Franco Ferrarotti, *Trattato di sociologia* (Turin: Utet, 1968).

Franco Ferrarotti, *Macchina e uomo nella società industriale* (Turin: ERI, 1970).

Franco Ferrarotti, *Per conoscere Pareto* (Milan: Mondadori, 1973).

Franco Ferrarotti, *Idee per la nuova società* (Florence: Vallecchi, 1974).

Franco Ferrarotti, *The Hypnotic Power of Violence* (Chieti: Human Science Paperback Solfanelli, 2016). (*L'ipnosi della violenza*, Milan: Rizzoli, 1980).

Franco Ferrarotti, *La tentazione dell'oblìo* (Rome-Bari: Laterza, 1985). (*The Temptation to Forget: Racism, Anti-semitism, Neo-Nazism*, Westport: Greenwood Press, 1994).

Franco Ferrarotti, *Storia e storie di vita* (Rome-Bari: Laterza, 1995).

Franco Ferrarotti, *Lineamenti di storia del pensiero sociologico* (Rome: Donzelli, 2002).

Hans Georg Gadamer, *Verità e Metodo*, It. transl., (Milan: Bompiani, 1996) (*Wahrheit und Methode*, 1986-1993).

Umberto Galimberti, *Psiche e techné. L'uomo nell'età della tecnica* (Milan: Feltrinelli, 1999).

Anthony Giddens, *The Consequences of modernity* (Stanford: Stanford University Press, 1991).

Ernst H. Gombrich, Julian Hochberg, Max Black, *Arte, Percezione, Realtà* (Turin: Einaudi, 1978-1992).

David Harvey, *The Condition of Postmodernity* (London, Hobocken NJ: Wiley-Blackwell, 1990).

Arnold Hauser, *Philosophie der Kunstgeschichte* (München: Beck, 1958).

Arnold Hauser, *Soziologie der Kunst* (München: Beck, 1974).

Fredric Jameson, *Postmodernism, or the Cultural Logic of Late Capitalism* (Durham: Duke University Press, 1984).

Jean-François Lyotard, *La condition postmoderne* (Paris: Editions de Minuit, 1979).

Herbert Marcuse, The Aesthetic Dimension. Toward a Critique of Marxist Aesthetics (Boston: Beacon Press, 1978)

Edgar Morin, *Le paradigme perdu: la nature humaine* (Paris: Editions du Seuil, 1973).

Nietzsche Friedrich, *Al di là del bene e del male*, It. transl., (Milan: Adelphi, 1968, 1977) (*Jenseits von Gut und Böse*).

Friederich Nietzsche, *Sull'utilità e il danno della storia per la vita*, It. transl., (Milan: Adelphi, 1973 and 1974) (*Unzeitgemässe Betrachtungen, Zweites Stück: Vom Nutzen und Nachteil der Historie für das Leben*).

Vilfredo Pareto, *Trattato di Sociologia Generale*, vols. I-II, (Milan: ed. Comunità, 1981).

Mario Perniola, *L'arte e la sua ombra* (Turin: Einaudi, 2000).

Franco Rella, *Il Silenzio e le Parole. Il pensiero nel tempo della crisi* (Milan: Feltrinelli, 1981).

Franco Rella, *Metamorfosi. Immagini del pensiero* (Milan: Feltrinelli, 1984).

Marco Sambin, *Arte e percezione visiva. Indicazioni per una metodologia nell'analisi del grado di realtà in arte*, in L. Pizzo Russo (ed.), "Estetica e Psicologia" (Bologna: il Mulino, 1982).

Georg Simmel, *Il conflitto della civiltà moderna* (Turin: Bocca ed., 1925).

Georg Simmel, *La metropoli e la vita mentale*, in C.W. Mills, *Immagini dell'uomo. La tradizione classica della sociologia* (Milan: ed. Comunità, 1969).

Georg Simmel, *Saggi di estetica* (Padua: Liviana Ed., 1970).

Georg Simmel, *Arte e civiltà* (Milan: ISEDI, 1976).

Georg Simmel, *La legge individuale e altri saggi* (Parma: Nuove Pratiche ed., 1995).

Georg Simmel, *Soziologie. Untersuchungen über die Formen der Vorgesellschaftung* (Leipzig: Duncker & Humblot, 1983).

Alfred Schütz, *Saggi Sociologici* (Turin: UTET, 1979).

Gianni Vattimo, *Tecnica ed esistenza* (Turin: Paravia, 1997).

Max Weber, *Wirtschaft und Gesellschaft* (Tübingen: Mohr, 1922).

Max Weber, *Gesammelte Aufsätze zur Wissenschaftslehre* (Tübingen: Mohr, 1922).

Simone Weil, *Réflexions sur les causes de la liberté et de l'oppression sociale* (Paris: Gallimard, 1955).

Historical and Political References

Riccardo Bauer, *Alla ricerca della libertà* (Florence: Parenti, 1957.

Giuseppe Colombo, *Industria e politica nella storia d'Italia* (Bari-Rome: Laterza, 1985).

Renzo De Felice (ed.), *Futurismo, Cultura e Politica* (Turin: Fondazione Giovanni Agnelli, 1986).

Renzo De Felice, *Mussolini il rivoluzionario* (Turin: Einaudi, 1965).

Alain Dewerpe, *Verso l'Italia industriale*, in *Storia of economia italiana*. Vol. III *L'età contemporanea: un paese nuovo* (Turin: Einaudi, 1991), pp. 6-7.

Detlef Mühlberger, *The Social Basis of the European Fascist Movement* (London, New York, Sydney: Croom Helm, 1987).

Emilio Gentile, *Il mito dello stato nuovo dall'antigiolittismo al fascismo* (Bari-Rome: Laterza, 1982).

Erich Nolte, *Il fascismo nella sua epoca. I tre volti del fascismo* (Carnago: ed. Sugarco, 1993).
Giovanni Sabbatucci, Vittorio Vidotto, *Storia d'Italia. Guerre e Fascismo*, vol. 4, (Bari-Rome: Laterza, 1997).
Maurizio Serra, *La ferita della modernità* (Bologna: il Mulino, 1992).
Maurizio Serra, *Al di là della decadenza* (Bologna: il Mulino, 1994).
Paolo Sylos Labini, *Saggio sulle classi sociali* (Bari-Rome: Laterza, 1974).

Cultural and Social Studies

Gottfried Benn, *Lo smalto sul nulla* (Milan: Adelphi, 1992).
Pierre Bourdieu, *L'amore dell'arte*, It. transl., (Rimini : Guaraldi, 1972) (*L'amour de l'art. Les musées d'art européens et leur public*, 1969).
Pierre Bourdieu, *Les Règles de l'Art. Genèse et structure du Champ littéraire* (Paris: Seuil, 1992).
Peter Bürger, *Teoria dell'avanguardia* (Turin: Bollati Boringhieri, 1990).
Peter Bürger, *La prose de la modernité*, Fr. transl., (Paris: Klincksieck, 1994) (*Prosa der Moderne*, 1988).
James Clifford, *The Predicament of Culture* (Harvard: Harvard University Press, 1988).
Gilles Deleuze, Felix Guattari, *Nomadologia. Pensieri per il mondo che verrà* (Rome: Castelvecchi, 1995).
John Dewey, *L'arte come esperienza*, It. transl., (Florence: La Nuova Italia, 1951) (*Art as Experience*, 1934).
Jean Duvignaud, *Sociologie de l'Art* (Paris: PUF, 1967).
Jean Duvignaud, *Sociologie du Théâtre* (Paris: PUF, 1965).
Mike Featherstone, *La cultura dislocata* (Rome: SEAM, 1998).
Franco Ferrarotti, in *La lente e lo specchio,* ed. Jader Jacobelli (Bari-Rome: Laterza, 1994).
James Joll, *Intellectuals in Politics. Three biographical essays* (London: Weidenfeld and Nicolson, 1960).
Ernst Jünger, *Al muro del Tempo* (Milan: Adelphi, 2000).
Lucien Goldmann, *La création culturelle dans la société moderne* (Paris: Denoel, 1971).
Erwin Panofsky, *Meaning in the Visual Arts. Papers in and on Art History* (New York: Anchor Books, 1955)
Ezio Raimondi, *Le poetiche della modernità* (Milan: Garzanti, 1990).

Reiner M. Rilke, *Elegie Duinesi* (Rome: Ed. B.M. Italiane, 1937).

Tzvetan Todorov, (ed.), *I Formalisti Russi* (Turin: Einaudi, 1968).

Vera L. Zolberg, *Constructing a Sociology of the Arts* (Cambridge: Cambridge University Press, 1990)

Futurist Writings

Guillaume Apollinaire, *Lettere a F.T. Marinetti*, P.A. Jannini (ed. by), (Fiesole: "Le Coste", 1978).

Umberto Boccioni, *Pittura e scultura futuriste* (Milan: SE, 1997).

Umberto Boccioni, *Grande Esposizione. Boccioni Pittore e Scultore Futurista* (Florence: SPES, 1916).

Bruno Corra, Emilio Settimelli, *Marinetti Intimo* (Milan: Sonzogno, 1911).

Bruno Corra, Emilio Settimelli, *Il teatro sintetico futurista* (Milan, 1915).

Maria Goretti, *La donna e il Futurismo* (Verona: La Scaligera, 1941).

Filippo Tommaso Marinetti, *Enquête Internationale sur Le Vers Libre* (Milan : Ed. Futuriste di "Poesia", 1909).

Filippo Tommaso Marinetti, *Le Futurisme* (Paris: Ed. Sansot et C.ie, 1911).

Filippo Tommaso Marinetti, *Come si seducono le donne e si tradiscono gli uomini* (Milan: Sonzogno, 1912).

Filippo Tommaso Marinetti, *Noi Futuristi* (Milan: Quinteri ed., 1917).

Filippo Tommaso Marinetti, *Lussuria-Velocità* (Milan: Modernissima, 1921).

Filippo Tommaso Marinetti, *Teoria e invenzione futurista* (Milan: Mondadori, 1968).

Filippo Tommaso Marinetti, *Collaudi Futuristi*, Viazzi Glauco (ed.), (Napoli: Guida, 1977).

Filippo Tommaso Marinetti, Aldo Palazzeschi, *Carteggio* (Milan: Mondadori, 1978).

Filippo Tommaso Marinetti, *Taccuini 1915/1921* (Bologna: il Mulino, 1987).

Giovanni Papini, *Il Mio Futurismo* (Florence: Edizioni di "Lacerba", 1914).

Giovanni Papini, *L'altra metà* (Florence: Vallecchi, 1922).

Giovanni Papini, *Diario* (Florence: Vallecchi ed., 1962).

Emilio Settimelli, *Inchieste sulla vita italiana* (Rocca S. Casciano, 1919).

Emilio Settimelli, *Marinetti. L'uomo e l'artista* (Milan: Edizioni Futuriste di "Poesia", 1921).

Studies of Avant-garde Art and Futurism

Vv Aa, *Literature and Revolution* (Boston: Beacon Press, 1967).

Alberto Abruzzese, *Forme estetiche e società di massa* (Venice: Marsilio, 1973).

Alberto Abruzzese, *Futurism e politica*, in "Art e Dossier" no. 2, *Il Futurismo*, M. Calvesi, E. Coen (ed.).

Umberto Artioli (ed.), *Il viandante e la sua orma* (Bologna: Cappelli, 1981).

Daniela Bertasio, *Professione Artista* (Bologna: Cluep, 1997).

Angelo Bozzolla, Caroline Tisdall, *Futurism*, It. transl., (Milan: Rusconi, 1988) (*Futurism*, 1977).

Cesare Brandi, *La fine dell'avanguardia e l'arte d'oggi* (Milan: ed. della Meridiana, 1952).

Omar Calabrese, *Il linguaggio dell'arte* (Milan: Bompiani, 1985).

Maurizio Calvesi, *Avanguardia di massa* (Milan: Feltrinelli, 1978).

Maurizio Calvesi, *Marinetti, inventore dell'avanguardia*, in *Marinetti e il Futurismo*, Catalogue (Rome: De Luca, 1994).

Antonio Castronuovo, *Il Futurismo a Imola* (Imola: Editrice La Mandragora, 1998).

Jean Clair, *La responsabilité de l'artiste* (Paris: Gallimard, 1997).

Guy Debord, *La Société du Spectacle* (Paris: Gallimard, 1992) (Paris: Buchet-Chastel, 1967).

Matteo D'Ambrosio, *Le commemorazioni in avanti di F.T. Marinetti* (Napoli: Liguori, 1999).

Mario De Micheli, *Le avanguardie artistiche del Novecento* (Milan: Feltrinelli, 1959).

Maria Drudi Gambillo, Teresa Fiori (ed.), *Archivi del Futurismo*, voll. I-II, (Rome: De Luca, 1962).

Carlo Ferrucci, *L'indicibile Sapere. Arte e realtà in Freud* (Rome: ed. Kappa, 1982).

Pierre Francastel, *Il futurismo e il suo tempo* (Paris: Sorbonne, 1965).

Donna Haraway, *Simians, Cyborgs, and Women. The Reinvention of Nature* (London: Free Associations Book, 1991).

Marcel Jean, *Autobiografia del Surrealismo* (Rome: Ed. Riuniti, 1983).

Giorgio Kaisserlian, *Vecchia e Nuova Avanguardia*, in "Contributi Martiniani".

Wassily Kandinsky, *Punto Linea Superficie*, It. transl., (Milan: Adelphi, 1968).

Rosalind Krauss, *Passaggi. Storia della scultura da Rodin alla Land Art* (Milan: Mondadori, 1998).

Eberhard Lämmert, Giorgio Cusatelli & Heinz-Georg Held, *Avantgarde, Modernität, Katastrophe. Letteratura, Arte, Scienza fra Germania e Italia nel Primo '900* (Florence: Leo S. Olschki, 1996).

Giovanni Lista, *Arte e Politica* (Milan: Multhipla, 1980).

Giovanni Lista, *Lo spettacolo futurista* (Florence: Cantini, 1990).

Giovanni Lista (ed.), *Enrico Prampolini. Carteggio Futurista* (Rome: Carte Segrete, 1992).

Giorgio Luti, *Firenze corpo 8* (Florence: Vallecchi, 1983).

Renato Poggioli, *Teoria dell'arte d'avanguardia* (Bologna: il Mulino, 1962).

Giuseppe Raimondi, *Gli archivi del futurismo*, in "Comunità" (Milan: October 1959).

Claudia Salaris (ed.), *F.T. Marinetti. Arte-Vita* (Rome: Fahrenheit 451, 1995).

Luis Mario Schneider, *México y el Surrealismo (1925-1950)* (Mexico: Arte y Libros, 1978).

Luigi Scrivo, *Sintesi del Futurismo. Storia e Documenti* (Rome: Bulzoni, 1968).

Lorenzo Taiuti, *Arte e media* (Genoa: Costa & Nolan, 1996).

Nico Stringa, *"...l'amato fecondo Manifesto": cenni sulla diffusione del Futurismo in Italia nel febbraio del 1909*, in "Futurismo. 1909-1944", (Milan: Mazzotta, 2001),

Karel Teige, *Il Mercato dell'arte* (Turin: Einaudi, 1973).

Karel Teige, *Arte e ideologia* (Turin: Einaudi, 1982).

Walter Vaccari, *Vita e tumulti di F.T. Marinetti* (Milan: Omnia Ed., 1959).

Lea Vergine, *Schegge* (Milan: Skira, 2001).

Lea Vergine, *Interrotti transiti* (Milan: Rizzoli, 2001).

Alberto Viviani, *Origini del nuovo spirito italiano* (Rome: Tosi, 1942).

Alberto Viviani, *Il poeta Marinetti e il Futurismo* (Turin: Paravia, 1940).

Theatre Studies

Giuseppe Bartolucci, *Il gesto futurista* (Rome: Bulzoni, 1969).

Achille Mango, *Verso una sociologia del teatro* (Rome: Celebes, 1978).

Mario Verdone, *Avventure teatrali del Novecento* (Soveria Mannelli: Rubbettino, 1999).

Reviews

Umberto Boccioni, *Il cerchio non si chiude*, in "Lacerba", 1 March 1914.

Anton Giulio Bragaglia, *La Fotografia del movimento (La fotodinamica futurista)*, in "Noi e il mondo", year III, no. 1, monthly magazine of "La Tribuna", Rome, January 1913.

Franco Ferrarotti, *Vilfredo Pareto: the disenchanted world of conservative pessimism*, An International Review, vol. 6, no. 2, Spring 1986.

Giovanni Lista, *Marinetti tra simbolismo e futurismo*, in "Primafila" a monthly periodical on theatre and live performance, no. 7, May 1995, pp. 43-44.

Giovanni Papini, *Cerchi aperti*, in "Lacerba", 15 March 1914.

Sergio Romano, *La cultura europea tra Otto e Novecento. Religione, Arte, Politica*, in "Nuova Storia Contemporanea", Anno V, n. 5, September-October 2001, (Florence: Le Lettere, 2001).

Ardengo Soffici, *Il soggetto nella pittura futurista*, in "Lacerba", 1 January 1914.

Newspapers

Franco Ferrarotti, *Chi ha messo la trappola in cui cadono i giovani?* in "Corriere della Sera", 15 April 1977.

Enrico Filippini, in response to Lucio Villari, *Dada: la sua negazione non è mai finita...*, in "La Repubblica", 21 December 1976.

Filippo Tommaso Marinetti, *Il Teatro di Varietà*, in "Daily-Mail", 21 November 1913.

Lucio Villari, *Dada contro tutti nell'Europa in guerra*, in "La Repubblica", 15 December 1976.

Encyclopaedias

Enrico Castelnuovo, Ilaria Bignamini, *Arte e Società*, in *Enciclopedia delle Scienze Sociali*, vol. I (Rome: Istituto della Enciclopedia Giovanni Treccani, 1991).

Paolo Bairoch, *Le politiche commerciali in Europa dal 1815 al 1914*, in *Storia Economica Cambridge. Le economie industriali*, vol. 8, (Turin: Einaudi, 1992).

Valerio Castronovo (ed.), *Storia Economica Cambridge*, vol. 8, (Turin: Einaudi, 1992).

Futurist Manifestos per year of Pubblication

Filippo Tommaso Marinetti, Manifesto del Futurismo, 20 Febbraio, 1909, "Le Figaro".

Francesco Balilla Pratella, *Manifesto tecnico*, 29 March 1911.

Filippo Tommaso Marinetti, *Manifesto dei Drammaturghi Futuristi*, 11 January 1911.

Giacomo Balla, *Manifesto dei pittori Futuristi*, Florence 1912.

Valentine de Saint-Point, *Manifesto della Lussuria*, 11 January 1913.

Carlo Carrà, *La pittura dei suoni, rumori e odori*, 13 August 1913.

Bruno Corradini, Emilio Settimelli, *Pesi, misure e prezzi del genio artistico*, Milan, 11 March 1914.

Giacomo Balla, Fortunato Depero, *La ricostruzione futurista dell'universo*, 11 March 1915.

Filippo Tommaso Marinetti, *La nuova religione-morale della velocità*, Milan, 11 May 1916.

Catalogues

Futurismo, 1909-1944 (Milan: Mazzotta, 2001), Enrico Crispolti (ed.).

Archivi del Futurismo (Rome: De Luca, 1962), Maria Drudi Gambillo (ed.).

Il Futurismo attraverso la Toscana (Livorno: Silvana ed., 2000) Enrico Crispolti (ed.).

Futuristi alla Spezia (La Spezia: ed. Tridente, 1991).

Futurismo & Futurismi (Milan: Bompiani, 1986) Pontus Hultén (ed.).

Printed by Agrisys Holding SA - in March 2019